Cooking with Noni

Recipes & Stories

Pauline Smarrella Lane

INTERROBANG COLLECTIVE

Cooking with Noni: Recipes and Stories

©2014 Pauline Smarrella Lane

ISBN: 978-0-615-98813-9

Image credits:

pg 62: "Shellfish in Bohol, Philippines" http://commons.wikimedia.org/wiki/File:Shellfish.jpg by pinay06 is licensed under CC by GNU Free documentation Licence, version 1.2
pg 63: "Shrimp Bisque/Bisque de Crevettes" http://commons.wikimedia.org/wiki/File:Shrimp_Bisque.jpg by French Recipes is licensed under CC by ShareAlike 3.0
pg 64: "Yellow Onions" http://commons.wikimedia.org/wiki/File:YellowOnions.jpg by Jon Sullivan has been released into the public domain by its author and copyright holder and licensed under CC by CC0
pg 74: "Dungeness Crabs" http://commons.wikimedia.org/wiki/File:Dungeness_crabs.jpg by John Sullivan has been released into the public domain by its author and copyright holder and licensed under CC by CC0
pg 99: "Pomme de Terre" http://commons.wikimedia.org/wiki/Potato#mediaviewer/File:Pomme_de_terre_vari%C3%A9t%C3%A9_bonnotte.JPG by BastienM is licensed under CC by CC-BY-SA-3.0,2.5,2.0,1.0, GFDL, License migration redundant

Interrobang Collective
www.InterrobangCollective.com

Printed in the United States of America

Cover design by Lorna Nakell

Cover and interior illustrations by Lorna Nakell

Interior design by Lorna Nakell and Poppy Milliken

For my family.

Table of Contents

Recipes

A VERY LIMITED EDITION

Fifteen years ago I put together a cookbook. It was a very tiny thing, six inches by eight inches and twenty-some pages thick. I painstakingly typed the recipes, ensuring that each one fit onto the half sized format. I used heavy cover paper for the front and back and sewed the whole thing together using a twig on the left side and heavy thread to bind it.

In the next few years, I put together about 30 cookbooks, which served as my primitive Christmas gifts and gifts for my volunteers at the food pantry. The recipients of these little books told me that they used the recipes all the time and that made me happy.

Over the years I would tell stories to my family and friends – pretty much to anyone who would listen. Recently my daughter Joan had her own Storycorps project, recording me and Jim talking about our lives before and after we were married. This is an important legacy for anyone. It is more than a family tree and it is indestructible. Our girls loved it and wanted more, and so, with encouragement from them and my husband Jim, and after years of procrastinating, I got on with it.

This is it and, of course, I hope you like it and that you enjoy the stories and find pleasure in the time you spend in your kitchen. Perfection is overrated so don't burden yourself with that. Turn on the music, lick some batter, eat a warm cookie right from the oven, crunch a crouton, punch down your bread dough and relax.

MAKING MY WAY

This is the picture that hangs on the wall behind my stove. It was taken in the kitchen at my grandfather's house and the woman who is working in this alley—like space of wooden counters and a sink is Grandpa's second wife. Her name was Olympia but everyone called her Limbutch and she married my grandfather a few years after my grandmother passed away.

She was a widow before that marriage and had been living with my parents, my two sisters and me. I was the reason she was there because she would be my caregiver for the first three and a half years of my childhood.

I didn't see her as often after she moved to my grandfather's house and she passed away when I was eight so my memories of Limbutch have been gathered mostly from pictures of her holding me and holding me so incessantly that, in later years, my Dad would laugh and say that I didn't walk until I was four.

When I see this picture of her working in such a primitive space I know that she would be astounded to see the conveniences that surround me in my kitchen. My appreciation for my good fortune is boundless.

It was out of necessity that I began to do some serious cooking. I grew up in a very ethnic steel town in Ohio populated by Italians, Poles, Greeks and Irish who had come in waves to work in the mills there. My family attended an Italian church and as children we went to the Italian parish school. In my class there were only two kids who were what we thought of as American.

We socialized mostly with other Italians who were from families who came from the same regions of Italy as our grandparents. Their food with its soul stirring smells and tastes was at every gathering and I took it all for granted. I went through an assimilation crisis—wishing I was blond and blue eyed and wanting to eat Wonder Bread covered with peanut butter and jelly.

When I went away to college I majored for a short time in Home Ec which included a Foods component as a preparation for a career in Dietetics. I stuck with it and the Clothing classes for two years and then fell under the spell of the Kennedy campaign. I switched to Economics and Political Science and spent more time on campaigning than on my studies.

Then came graduate school at West Virginia University where I met Bucky (Jim), the Anglo Saxon, married him and had three adorable little girls in four years. I remained a political junkie but, as time went on, I also became more and more a cooking junkie.

We moved to Oregon a year after Piper Aircraft Corporation sent Bucky to the Northwest as a District Manager. Our first child, Cristianne, was one and a half, our second, Kathleen, was on the way. And after that, in a little over four years of marriage, we had our third and last baby, Joan.

Our new environment was so different that it seemed like it might be the closest I would come to living in a foreign country. Joan, in second grade, informed me that Italians came from Italy. "Where did you think they came from?" I asked. She said, "I thought they came from Ohio". I couldn't have expressed it better, such was the dichotomy. I loved Eugene but it was a wasteland as far as anything Italian was concerned.

On my biennial trips to Ohio my Dad would take me to the Italian store before I returned to Oregon and he would buy me sauces, pasta, salami, pepperoni and hard cheeses. We would pack a big cardboard box for me to take home on the airplane—restrictions being almost non-existent then. Once, at the check-in counter, the agent asked what was in the box—a standard question—and I said it was food. He asked, "Are you Italian?" Aha! He had met others out there who had to lug their precious food around with them.

I had learned some skills when I was young but they were mostly kitchen helper duties. I remember sealing the ravioli with a fork, rolling each of the gnocchi to create a little pocket, popping the skins off of the ceci (garbanzos), and pinching the tops off the parsley to store in a jar in the refrigerator. These are all things I still do but I really had to learn much more so that I could survive the time between my visits to Ohio.

My parents came every other year and I asked my mother to show me just one thing each time—gnocchi, ravioli, pizza, pizzelles. And, though I didn't master these dishes immediately, I kept at it until I did. Then one day, sometime in the 70's, I stumbled onto a cooking show on public television called The Romagnoli's Table. What a joy it was for me to be able to watch Franco, who was obviously from Southern Italy, cooking the food that I knew so well. He made it look easy and I watched him whenever I could and ordered his book. It was published in 1974 and when it was updated years later I bought a copy for each of my girls.

I needed to have the food of my ancestors and I needed to cook it myself. I had an advantage since I knew what a dish was supposed to look like and how it should taste. And so with time and practice my results gradually became more authentic and satisfying to me.

Over the years I felt confident enough to teach Italian cooking classes and I also cooked at a soup kitchen and for a few months at a sorority house. I worked at a restaurant long enough to pick up tips on catering and I became a sometime caterer. I learned about cooking and also things about life from all of these experiences and I value it all.

I have passed along many tried and true recipes to my daughters and to countless friends and I probably tired them out with stories that, at least to me, were funny and crazy and often bittersweet. I hope that this compilation will be helpful and enjoyable for you.

Appetizers

Blue Cheese Grapes

Note:

You may be able to find canned almonds at the market already chopped and possibly toasted. Otherwise, finely chop them, spread on a baking sheet and toast at 350 for about 10 minutes. Watch closely because it's a quick trip from toasted to burnt.

This appetizer looks great, tastes great and will be a nice surprise for your guests. It may sound a bit involved but if you break down the preparation over a few days, it is quite easy.

You Will Need:

4 ounces blue cheese, crumbled

8 ounces cream cheese, softened

1-2 tablespoons brandy

3 dozen red seedless grapes, washed and dried well

2 cups almonds, finely chopped and toasted

Mix blue cheese and cream cheese until very well combined. Add brandy to taste and blend it into the cheese mixture until it is very smooth. Chill until firm. This can be done a day or two ahead if you like.

On the day before serving, wrap a generous teaspoonful of the cream cheese around each grape and work it around, rolling a bit until it is smooth. Refrigerate the grapes, covered and in one layer overnight. At this time you can prepare the almonds and cover them tightly until ready to use.

A few hours before serving, roll each grape in the chopped nuts so they are completely covered. Refrigerate them until ready to serve. They look pretty on their own plate or interspersed with a variety of other appetizers.

Blue Cheese Spread

Prepare this and you will have a very easy and beautiful addition to your appetizer table.

You Will Need:

16 ounces of cream cheese

8 ounces of blue cheese

2 cups sour cream, divided

3 large eggs

¼ teaspoon or less ground black pepper

1-2 tablespoons brandy (optional)

A few pounds of red seedless grapes, washed, dried and cut into small clusters

Assorted crackers or bread rounds

Chopped walnuts for garnish

In a large mixer bowl, beat the cream cheese and blue cheese until fluffy. Add one cup of sour cream and blend well. Add eggs and beat just until well combined. Mix in a little black pepper to taste. You can also add the brandy at this time if you choose.

Pour into a lightly oiled 9" springform pan. Place this on a cookie sheet and bake at 325 for 25-30 minutes or until lightly golden brown. Remove it from the oven and let stand for about 5 minutes. Top with a generous cup of sour cream, spreading it to about ½" from edge.

Return to oven for another 5 minutes or until set. Let cool and then refrigerate, covered, overnight.

To serve, run a sharp knife around side of the pan, remove sides and place spread in the center of a tray that is large enough to have about 5-6 inches to spare around the edge. Scatter chopped walnuts around outer edge of the sour cream topping. Then, dividing the spread into thirds (just in your mind's eye), place small clusters of red seedless grapes falling off the edge in a cascading manner in three places. Within the divisions, on the tray, arrange crackers of your choice.

Note:

If I am having a small party, I bake this spread in two small springform pans. I freeze one and serve the other. Check a pan substitution chart to find out which small pans will add up to the same amount of batter as the one large one. Baking time may be a little less in the smaller pans.

Marinated Red Peppers

Note:

For later use, put serving size amounts of roasted peppers into zip bags, remove any air and freeze. Do not marinate before freezing. Drain them when thawed and blot off any excess moisture. Cut them into desired size and add the other ingredients.

This is a very traditional dish that can be served as an appetizer or with dinner or used as an addition to a frittata or a panini or as topping for a pizza. The recipe is only about the preparation. You can decide on the amount you would like to prepare. Take advantage of the end of summer produce markets to buy a large quantity of the peppers at a good price and quality. You can freeze them after roasting and finish them off when ready to use.

You Will Need:

Red roasting peppers

Garlic

Fresh parsley

Extra virgin olive oil

Salt and pepper

To roast the peppers, line a jelly roll pan with foil and place whole red bell peppers on it. Slide the pan onto an oven rack positioned so that the peppers will be an inch under the broiler, checking them often and turning them as they blacken.

A quicker way to do a large quantity of the peppers is to set your out-door grill on high heat and place the peppers directly on oiled racks, turning as they blacken. Put the peppers in a bowl as they are removed from the heat and cover tightly with foil while the others are blackening. Let them all cool off a little so you can handle them. Peel the skins off under a tiny stream of cold water and remove the core and the seeds. Quarter them, drain well and let them completely cool. Lay them out on paper towels to remove any water that is still clinging to them.

To serve, cut the peppers into strips or squares or sizes that will work with your plans. Place the pieces in a bowl and pour enough olive oil over them to coat them nicely, but not so they are swimming in the oil. Add slivers of garlic and finely chopped parsley and salt and pepper. Adjust amounts to suit your taste but remember, the peppers should be the dominant flavor. Marinate them at room temperature for several hours before serving. A nice presentation is a small bowl of peppers on a platter with crunchy toasted Italian bread and a few wedges of soft cheese.

Caponata

This is a lightly flavored dish and not a difficult one but there is a bit of time involved—mostly for the chopping.

You Will Need:

1 medium size eggplant

½ cup of roasted red peppers

Generous ½ cup pitted green olives

½ cup diced onions

4-5 cloves garlic, minced

2 tablespoons olive oil

¼ cup chopped fresh parsley

2 tablespoons capers, roughly chopped

Juice of ½ a large lemon

Slice the stem end off the eggplant and discard. Cut little slits all over the remaining eggplant with a small paring knife and rub all over with olive oil. Place it on an oiled foil lined pan and roast in a 400 oven for about 45 minutes. Baking time may vary with the circumference of the eggplant.

Test the eggplant for doneness by lightly squeezing it to make sure it is soft inside. Peel the skin off and let it cool a bit. Dice it and the peppers and olives and place into a large bowl. You could do this in a food processor if you are very careful to just pulse it a few times. You don't want to puree it.

While the eggplant mixture is cooling saute onions and garlic in 2 tablespoons of olive oil until lightly golden. Cool a little and add to eggplant mixture along with parsley, salt, pepper, lemon juice and capers.

Serve with crackers, pita or toasted garlic bread.

Note:

If you are preparing this the day before, cover and refrigerate and then bring to room temperature before serving. If you fix it early in the day of serving it will be fine if you just set it aside until needed.

Stuffed Mushrooms

This is a very simple and good basic recipe, one that emphasizes the taste of the mushrooms. Much of it can be prepared in advance so you will only need a few minutes to finish it off before baking. Use large but not giant mushrooms.

You Will Need:

12 large white or brown mushrooms, cleaned, with stems popped off and reserved

3 green onions, finely chopped

1 large garlic clove, finely chopped

3 tablespoons olive oil plus an additional ¼ cup for oiling the caps

3 tablespoons butter

2 tablespoons minced fresh parsley or 2 teaspoons dried

3 tablespoons finely grated Parmesan or Romano

⅓ cup seasoned bread crumbs or enough to absorb the liquid from cooking

Salt and pepper

Remove the stems from the mushrooms by popping them off, which will leave a little pocket in the cap to hold the stuffing. You may want to slice off and discard a small part of the bottom of the stem if it looks tough. Finely chop the stems along with the green onions and garlic clove. The food processor works well if you are careful to just pulse a few times. Saute this mixture in the olive oil and butter over medium high heat for about 5 minutes or until the onion is tender. Remove from heat and add the parsley, cheese and enough of the seasoned bread crumbs to absorb most of the moisture. Add salt and pepper to taste.

To bake, brush the outside of the caps with olive oil and fill cavity with a heaping spoonful of stuffing. Drizzle a little olive oil over top of each one and bake on a slightly oiled pan at 350 for 15-20 minutes.

Note:

To clean the mushrooms, use one of the soft brushes that are made for this. The white or brown mushrooms are grown in clean conditions and will not require washing. If you wet them they may be a bit slimy on the outside and the area under the cap can suck up water like a sponge.

The do aheads are: After cleaning and stemming the mushrooms, place caps in a paper bag with a slightly damp paper towel on top and refrigerate. Make stuffing and cover and refrigerate until ready to bake the mushrooms. About half an hour before serving brush the caps, fill them, drizzle oil on top, bake and serve while warm.

Mushroom Turnovers

If you enjoy working with pastry dough, this is a fun project. The kids can do the sealing and maybe some of the filling and folding too. It's a simple way to introduce them to cooking.

You Will Need:

8 ounces softened cream cheese

1 stick butter, softened

1 ½ cups all purpose flour

2 tablespoons flour

3 tablespoons butter

½ pound finely chopped mushrooms

½ medium onion, finely chopped

¼ cup sour cream

¼ teaspoon thyme

Salt to taste

1 egg, beaten with a teaspoon of water

With your mixer on medium speed beat the cream cheese and the butter until well combined. Add the 1½ cups flour and continue beating until it can be gathered into a ball. Flatten it into a disc, wrap tightly with plastic wrap and refrigerate for an hour or more.

Melt 3 tablespoons of butter in a skillet and add mushrooms and onions. Cook until tender. Remove from heat and stir in flour, sour cream, thyme and salt. Set aside until cooled.

Divide chilled dough in half and roll out ½" to about ⅛" thick. Using a round cutter or a glass cut circles that are about 2½" in diameter. Place a teaspoonful of the mushroom mixture on half of the circle and brush edges of dough with the beaten egg. Fold dough over and press edges together with a fork. Place on slightly greased cookie sheet and brush tops with some of the beaten egg. Cut a few small slits in top. Bake 12-14 minutes at 400 or until golden brown.

You will get about 3 dozen.

Note:

If freezing, place uncooked turnovers, without brushing them with egg, on a waxed paper lined cookie sheet and freeze until they are hard. Then store in zip bags. Partially thaw when ready to use, brush with egg wash and slit the top at this time. Bake a bit longer than 14 minutes.

Lotsa Chicken Wings

I think everyone loves chicken wings—I know I do—and these are easy to prepare. This is a good party recipe, enough for twenty or more servings. I usually cut it in half, especially when I am including other appetizers at the table.

You Will Need:

60 chicken wings

½ cup soy sauce

2 pounds of any combination of apricot, pineapple or orange marmalade

¼ cup sugar

1 large lemon, juiced and with zest finely grated

2 teaspoons ginger

1 teaspoon cinnamon

½ teaspoon nutmeg

1 teaspoon thyme

3-4 crushed garlic cloves

2 tablespoons orange juice

Cut the chicken wings into three pieces. Save the tip for later use in chicken stock and separate the rest of the wing at the joint. You will have 120 pieces.

Make the marinade: Combine all ingredients except the chicken in a saucepan and stir over low heat until sugar is dissolved and mixture is well blended.

Place wings in two lightly oiled large roasting pans. Bake for ½ hour at 375 and pour off any accumulated drippings. Set aside 1 cup of marinade and, using half of the remainder for each pan, spoon it over the wings. Bake for 1½ hours at 350, basting and turning frequently. You want a shiny coating that sticks to the wings. Add more sauce as necessary and watch closely so they don't brown too much.

Note:

For an even easier prep time, buy the frozen wings that are already separated. They are sold without the tip. Thaw and pat dry before using.

These can be made the day before and reheated, covered at 300 until warmed through. Use some of the reserved sauce if you need it at this time.

Smoked Salmon Spread

If I am having a big party with lots of dishes, I love having a few that I can prepare a day or two in advance. This fits that bill perfectly.

You Will Need:

8 ounces cream cheese at room temperature

½ cup sour cream (light will work)

1 tablespoon fresh lemon juice

1 scant tablespoon dill weed

1 tablespoon minced chives

2 teaspoons creamy horseradish

Salt and pepper to taste

4 ounces minced smoked salmon

In large mixer bowl cream the cheese until it is smooth. Add the sour cream, dill, lemon juice, horseradish and salt and pepper. Mix until well blended. Add the salmon and mix thoroughly. Chill and serve with crackers or crudites.

Note:

If making this ahead, remove from the refrigerator about an hour before serving so that it is slightly softened.

Corn & Wild Rice Pancakes with Smoked Salmon

Note:

Unless you use wild rice regularly, you can buy the little you need for this recipe at the bulk food section of your grocery store. Follow the directions on the bin as different varieties may require different cooking times.

At one of the Portland Farmer's Markets I watched a cooking demonstration by a young chef from Zinc Bistro. I have simplified his recipe a bit, substituting a good quality store bought jam for a homemade one and using sour cream instead of crème fraiche. It is a pretty and delicious appetizer and I've always had rave reviews when I serve it.

You Will Need:

For the Pancakes:

1½ cups flour

½ teaspoon salt

1½ teaspoon baking powder

3 eggs, separated

1½ cups milk (whole or 2%)

¾ cup cooked corn (fresh or frozen kernels), blanched and chopped a bit

¾ cup cooked wild rice

For the assembly:

Thinly sliced smoked salmon

Sour cream

Blackberry or huckleberry preserves

To prepare the pancakes, sift together the flour, salt and baking powder. Add the egg yolks and milk. Stir in corn and wild rice. Fold in 3 stiffly beaten egg whites. Cook as you would any pancakes, keeping the batter thicker than a crepe but still a bit thinner than a regular pancake. About 1½" in diameter. They can be made a few hours ahead and kept covered at room temperature. To assemble, layer thinly sliced smoked salmon on top of the pancake, then a small teaspoon of sour cream with a little jam on top.

DON

This is Don Johnson posing with a somewhat overgrown zucchini from his garden. He generously acted as my weekly greengrocer and he is also the reason that I ended up serving on the Board of the Community Family Soup Kitchens. He was one of the founders of that organization which was set up with the help of Ernie Unger who had operated the Eugene Mission for many years. Mr. Unger recognized the

need for a facility that would serve families, especially mothers and children who might be more comfortable in a different setting than the Mission could provide. At the CFSK the tables were set with flowers and there were games and books for the kids and volunteers from the Literacy Council who helped adults who had an interest in learning to read. It was a comforting environment.

As he did for every nonprofit that asked him, Don, the retired shop teacher, built shelves, picked up donated food and oversaw the everyday operation of the organization. There were four sites to be managed and at one point I became the cook at one of them. We were in need of someone to run one of the kitchens, two times a week, for less than a year and it wasn't feasible to hire one. Don asked me to step in and I am thankful I said yes.

I admit I was apprehensive at first because it meant cooking for about 50-60 people with ingredients that changed each week. We always could depend on boxes of distressed produce which our trusty volunteers turned into one huge bowl of green salad and one of fruit. We had a stock of canned vegetables and canned meat and a constant supply of Kentucky Fried Chicken. For dessert the grocery stores donated plenty of cakes and our supply of bread was overwhelming.

For me, the challenge was to turn out a healthful meal, one that I would feel good about serving to my family. The chicken might be served one night just as is but a more inviting offering might be a noodle casserole or a hearty soup with rice and vegetables. The bread could be sliced and buttered or turned into a bread pudding. I didn't realize the importance of that little extra effort until I saw the smiles as people came through the line. Several thanked me because it reminded them of their mother's cooking. It was touching.

Don would stop by often to bring salvaged groceries and one day he called and asked if I could use some potatoes. My rule was that I never turned anything down but I didn't know until he came that it was a truckload that had overturned on the highway. You might be surprised at how many things you can do with potatoes.

Many of the same families came to the site each time and we encouraged the volunteers to have dinner with them. You learn a lot over the dinner table. We didn't all have the same problems, of course, but we could find common ground. Don was the master of bridging the gap. He was soft spoken and kind and he could always tell a funny story or two. He passed away a few years ago and left a great big hole in the lives of many people.

If you have a generous friend who is supplying you with zucchini, here is one fun recipe for you.

Zucchini Sticks

You Will Need:

2-3 small zucchini

1 large egg beaten with a tablespoon of water

⅓ cup flour for dusting the zucchini

¾ cup seasoned bread crumbs

Oil to coat skillet to ½" (half canola and half olive oil)

Grated Parmesan (optional)

Cut each zucchini into 2½" chunks and cut each chunk lengthwise into spears a bit larger around than a pencil. Trim the seeds, if any, from the edge of each piece. You should get 12 spears from each zucchini. Drop them into a paper bag with the flour. Shake them up a bit, remove from bag and knock off any excess flour. Next dip the spears into beaten egg, then into the bread crumbs. Roll them in crumbs so that they are completely covered. Refrigerate in a single layer until ready to use. This can be done early in the day.

I recommend that you brown these right before serving. You will need to have your oil heated to somewhere right around medium high. You can test it with a small piece of the breaded zucchini. The end result should be a crisp, golden vegetable stick. If your oil is not hot enough the inside of the zucchini will be soft by the time the outside is golden. Avoid putting them in a low oven to keep warm because that will also further cook the insides. Better to serve them at warm or room temperature than to have them be mushy.

After they are golden and crisp remove to paper towels for a few minutes and transfer to serving plate. Sprinkle lightly with sea salt and, if you like, scatter some shredded Parmesan over the top. Serve immediately.

Zucchini Flowers

You Will Need:

12 flowers

2 eggs

1 tablespoon olive oil

⅔ cup warm water

¼ teaspoon salt

¾ cup flour

If you or your friends have zucchini in the garden, you can harvest the flowers that will not actually produce a vegetable. If you look closely, you will see that some of the flowers have a little bump at the base that will grow into a zucchini. If there is no bump the flower will eventually just wither. Pick them when they are closed but still fresh looking. You may be able to buy them at some of the farmers' markets or at a specialty market. Or be brave enough to ask gardening friends if you can raid their gardens since the bumpless flowers would most likely end up in the compost anyway.

To prepare, remove the pistils from the inside of the flower. Occasionally you may have to remove a wiggling green worm from inside, too. I think that is a good sign that there were no chemicals used on the garden! Gently brush or rinse off the flowers and dry carefully.

Make the Batter: Combine the rest of the ingredients, whisking so there are no lumps. It is good to allow batter to sit for an hour or so in order for it to become more homogeneous. You want it to be thick enough to cling to the flowers but not quite as heavy as pancake batter.

To Cook: Gently dip the flowers, a few at a time, in the batter, and then fry them until they are golden in a deep saucepan with about 2 inches of vegetable oil. Medium high usually works well, but every stove is different. Adjust the heat so that they cook quickly enough to avoid absorbing oil. Do not crowd the pan and turn once to make sure they are golden colored on both sides. Drain on paper towels and keep warm in a very low oven (200) while finishing all. Sprinkle with a little sea salt before serving.

Note:

All of us have cooked our share of zucchini and my experience has been that I am never using the vegetable without adding some herbs or onion and garlic to complement its very delicate flavor. The flowers are a different product and they are delicious when prepared with a very plain and simple batter. This is one of my favorite dishes but the blossoms are hard to come by, not nearly as plentiful as the zucchini itself and definitely a seasonal commodity.

I prefer this very plain recipe but the flowers may also be stuffed with small bits of fresh mozzarella before dipping in the batter. You can also grate some Parmesan over top at serving time.

Note:

I am fortunate to have a good friend who has many fig trees on his property. He invited me to pick as many figs as I wanted before the birds got them.

Baked Wontons with Goat Cheese & Fig

I came up with this recipe when I was asked to provide appetizers and desserts for a fundraiser event in Portland. I was trying to stretch the budget as far as possible and this inexpensive appetizer turned out to be a big hit. The wontons were two dollars for a package of 40-50, and can be found in the freezer section at any Asian grocery store.

You will Need:

1 package wonton wrappers (the thin ones)

Goat cheese or boursin

1 small jar of fig preserves (recipe follows)

Sea Salt

Small sprigs of fresh rosemary

Cut the wontons in half so that you have 80 to 100 rectangles. Brush them lightly on both sides with olive oil and sprinkle with coarse salt. Bake in 375 oven until golden brown. You may have to turn them once.

They will curl slightly but they look pretty that way. If you are making them the day before, store them in a tightly closed bag until ready to use.

To serve, drop a teaspoon of the goat cheese onto a baked wonton and top with a bit of fig preserves (recipe follows) and then push a tiny sprig of rosemary into the topping. Arrange attractively on a large tray.

Fig Preseves

These preserves will keep in the refrigerator for only a month and should be frozen if you are keeping them longer than that.

You Will Need:

2 pounds light skinned, medium sized figs (20 or so), stemmed and quartered.

½ cup sugar

¼ cup water

¼ cup honey

¼ cup light corn syrup

2 tablespoons fresh lemon juice

⅛ teaspoon salt

Combine all ingredients in a medium sized saucepan. Bring to a boil over medium high heat. Reduce heat and simmer for about 50 minutes or until thick and syrupy, stirring occasionally. Remove from heat and let cool. You will get about 2½ cups which can be ladled into jars and refrigerated.

If you are unsure about the thickness, spoon a little on a saucer and place in the freezer for a few minutes to see if it has a jamlike consistency.

Note:

I did use the Adriatic figs, which are green skinned with white flesh and a pink seedy area. You could try Calimyrnas or others that are available. Figs are very expensive at the market so, if you don't get a bargain, buying the preserves may be a better option.

Oranges with Oil & Olives

Note:

The traditional version of this recipe often calls for the dry cured olives. I don't like them so I use Kalamatas. Try both and use what you like. Also, both the two types of oranges I have used are juicy and sweet. The navel is seedless and the Valencia has just a few seeds. Buy the ones that are in greater supply – that's a hint that they are in season somewhere and so they are usually sweeter.

I have used this recipe as an appetizer or as a side dish and also with a dessert buffet. It is one of the most popular recipes among my cooking class students. I think it works well at any time, is refreshing and contains an unusual combination of flavors. You can decide on the amounts you want to use. The recipe is mostly about the process.

You Will Need:

Oranges, navel or valencia

Olive Oil

Black olives dry cured, kalamata or your choice

Sea salt and freshly ground pepper

Using a very sharp knife, cut a small slice from the top and bottom of oranges. Standing an orange on end on your serving plate, remove the peel in a similar fashion as you would a pineapple. You must remove all of the white but try to not remove any of the actual meat of the fruit. By working on the plate you will not lose any of the juice. Cut slices a bit over ¼" and continue with other oranges. You usually can get 5 slices per orange.

Arrange the slices attractively on a platter and drizzle a few tablespoons of olive oil over the top. Sprinkle with salt and pepper and then scatter a few olives around and on top of the oranges.

Vegetables

MY GRANDFATHER'S GARDEN

When we moved to Oregon in 1966 we bought a house that sat on a half acre of ground with a beautifully manicured rose garden in the front yard. The back of the property was split by a massive laurel hedge which, if you were looking out the kitchen windows, hid three giant trees—one with apples, one with Royal Anne cherries and one with walnuts.

We lived there with one baby, then two, and then a third and so I didn't have the time or the knowledge to garden. However I did learn a few good things from the older women in the neighborhood. They told me our apples were Gravensteins and they gave me recipes for applesauce and apple squares. They laughed when I worried about picking all those walnuts from the tree and I was relieved when they said that the things that looked like little limes would split open and release the walnut inside. I would be able to pick them up and dry them on a rack by the furnace in the basement. And what would I do with the bumper crop of cherries? The ladies directed me to Brunner's Dryer, only a mile away, where I could actually sell them. We didn't spray our trees and some of the cherries had tiny worms but they bought them anyway, at a cheaper price, for the syrup that would be extracted for soft drinks and cough medicine. Really! I also became a pretty decent rose pruner and did my first cuts in late fall and my second in early spring. And the laurel hedge grew and grew and I trimmed it and trimmed it.

By 1969 we were outgrowing our two bedroom house and we heard through the grapevine that the big house directly behind us, with an acre of land that abutted the back of our property, was going to be for sale. After a short conversation of should we, shouldn't we, we knocked on the door of the house and introduced ourselves to the couple who, it turned out, were renting from an elderly relative. They told us that the house was drafty (true) and that it needed much work (true) and that they wouldn't recommend it to anyone. So we bought it.

We now had a back yard with a very big Gravenstein tree, a few plum and peach trees, a row of raspberry plants and lots of crazy out of control blackberries. It was blessed with rich soil left from the old river bed that many years ago had run through the area and was warmed by hours of sunshine at just the right time of day. All around us were people with gardens big and small but I had no idea of where to start with mine even though the Lane County Extension Service answered a question or two and the neighbors were kind and helpful.

Floating in the back of my mind were thoughts of my grandfather's garden. I wanted my garden to be like his and I had at least four times the amount of space that he had. Regretfully I didn't have much of a relationship with him because he spoke little English and I spoke no Italian and I was always too shy to try. And by the time I was ready to grow things he was old and sick and I lived two thousand miles away.

When Grandpa arrived in this country, he went to work at the steel mill – six days a week, 12 hours a day. He came from a small village in Italy and, as a boy, had tended sheep. In his new environment he was surrounded by the giant machinery of the mill and, strangely enough, he became the man to see when the equipment broke down. He could read the blueprints and figure out what was needed for the repair. The workers remembered him long after he retired.

I wish I could ask him now how, with work and family, he had time to grow a garden and cultivate his entire long and narrow yard all the way back to the alley. He had a Seckel pear tree and an arbor for his Concord grapes and even a fig tree that he covered and protected through the cold Ohio winters. There were tomatoes, peppers, onions, garlic, green beans, zucchini, eggplant, basil, oregano, parsley, too much to even remember. It was fascinating to me when, at the end of the season, he smashed the overripe tomatoes onto screens, dried them in the sun and harvested the little seeds that would become next summer's plants.

Grandpa's garden and an additional one that he tended on a vacant property helped to feed his family of nine and also the two boarders who had come from Italy to work in the mill. And later, while my Dad was away doing his residency, my mother and their first child moved in, along with the daughter-in-law's teenage brother who had nowhere else to go. I had no such challenges to meet. My garden was for my enjoyment and the satisfaction of the harvest.

So I plunged ahead with my plantings, with no rhyme nor reason to it, and I put in radishes first. I don't like radishes but on the seed envelope it said that they grew fast and I needed some instant gratification. I also liked surprises, so I tried things that I could pull from underground— carrots, onions, garlic and, later on, potatoes. Thinning the rows seemed wasteful to me so I ended up with some very tiny carrots. Tomatoes were my favorite because when they were ripe they smelled better than anything and just begged you to take a bite right there in the garden. I had beautiful bush beans and an eggplant that died an early death (story follows), too many zucchini plants and wheelbarrows full of corn.

Lucky for me that, right across the street, lived Olive and Marjorie, two elderly sisters who had retired from school teaching many years before. They knew almost as much as Grandpa did about growing things and preserving them and, one special day ,they taught me to shuck and blanch and cut the kernels from what seemed like a never ending pyramid of corn.

The small house that the sisters shared was situated on a large piece of land and, inside and out, they were dedicated to recycling almost everything. On the wooden chairs there were pads braided out of colorful plastic bread wrappers and the side tables held embroidered doilies made from pieces of old flour sacks. Their food waste was composted and one day I witnessed the most innovative recycling effort I had ever seen. Marjorie drove her VW bug onto the front lawn and, one bucketful at a time, carried out her used bath water. She washed her car with it and, as the water dripped down, at least a part of the lawn got some relief from the almost drought like conditions of our very hot summer. I can't say I followed her example but I sure thought it was a heck of an idea.

ONE FINE EGGPLANT

In the one and only summer in which I planted eggplant, it seemed that it took forever to flower and even longer to mature. From week to week I could barely see a difference. It was like watching hair grow. I finally had one eggplant, a lovely deep purple one, on the only plant that survived. The last time I saw it, it was about the size of a large pear. I was sitting in the sun on the front porch, enjoying a break, and Kathleen, who was four at the time, came around from the back yard and handed me something. "Is this ready yet?" she asked. I don't even remember what my answer was. I only recall her standing there so sweet and serious. My one and only eggplant would never be ready but that was some fine day. After that I bought my eggplants at the grocery store.

Grilled Eggplant

I prefer the deep purple ones. Sometimes they are long and slender and other times medium size and more rounded. Using a lengthwise cut on the fatter eggplants I can usually get 5-6 slices for the grill. One or two pieces per person is a good serving, especially if you have other vegetables with your meal.

You Will Need:

Eggplant

Olive oil

Salt

Cut an inch from the top of the eggplant. Slice the remainder, unpeeled, slightly on the diagonal and lay out on a large platter. You can overlap the slices but make sure they are all well sprinkled with salt. Let them rest for about 20 minutes as they bead up with moisture. You may rinse them VERY slightly and then pat dry with a paper towel. Brush one side with olive oil and place on an oiled grill that is pre-heated to medium. Watch closely so that they have nice grill lines on the bottom but are not black. Brush top of slices with oil and turn them and brown the other side. Remove to a serving platter and sprinkle lightly with sea salt.

Note:

It is not necessary to serve these right off the grill. They are fine at room temperature. For a beautiful and delicious vegetable offering you may want to create a colorful platter of grilled peppers, tomatoes, onions and Portobellos along with the eggplant.

Fried Eggplant

I have used this recipe forever. The small rounds work as an appetizer, the somewhat larger ones as a base for parmigiana or just as a side dish. As in the last recipe, the amounts vary with the size of the vegetable.

You Will Need:

1-2 eggplants, depending on size

Salt

Olive oil

Canola oil

2 eggs, beaten with a tablespoon of water

½ cup flour

First, cut about an inch off the top of the eggplant and peel the whole eggplant as you would a pineapple.

Slice into rounds about ¼" thick. Then, and here is the very important part, lay them in a shallow casserole and heavily salt each layer. Let this sit for 20-30 minutes after which there will be some liquid in the dish. Remove slices. Rinse them just a bit, lay them out on paper towels and pat them dry.

To cook, coat a large skillet with equal amounts of olive oil and vegetable oil to a depth of ¼". Heat to medium high. Place slices of eggplant in some flour and then shake off the excess. Dip them in the beaten egg, coating them completely and saute on both sides to a golden brown. Remove from skillet onto paper towels.

At this time, you have several options. You can serve them immediately or they can be done several hours ahead and served at room temperature. Or, you can freeze them for later use. To do this, stack them with plastic wrap in between each slice and place in freezer bag. They will be ready for later use in eggplant parmigiana or just as a side dish.

Note:

I cut a small piece from the end of the peeled eggplant and I flour and coat it with the egg wash and then use it to test the temperature of the oil. If the eggplant is cooking too slowly it will absorb oil, if too fast it will burn. You will learn to spot the difference with practice.

Eggplant Parmigiana

Note:

A good vegetarian option is to layer the eggplant with the mozzarella, some sliced cooked mushrooms or even some thinly sliced hard boiled eggs and, of course, the marinara.

You can adjust the recipe to serve a few people or a group.

You can make this dish with only the mozzarella and Parmesan and sauce or you can add one or two of the optional ingredients. If you are trying it for the first time, you may want to keep it simple so that you get the layering and the timing right.

You Will Need:

16 or more fried eggplant slices (see previous recipe)

2 cups or more marinara sauce (in entrée section of this book)

1½ cups coarsely shredded mozzarella

½ cup finely grated Parmesan or Romano

1 cup cooked tiny meatballs, about the size of a marble

1 cup cooked, sliced mushrooms, optional (recipe in appetizer section of book)

2 hard boiled eggs, thinly sliced (optional)

If you are using meatballs prepare them using ground beef seasoned only with salt and pepper. Brown them in an oiled pan over medium heat, shaking them around so they cook evenly. They will cook through very quickly. Remove from heat with a slotted spoon and set aside.

Lightly oil a shallow rectangular or oval baking dish or you can even use a pie plate. Using your cooked eggplant slices line the bottom and slightly up the sides of the casserole, overlapping enough to cover any holes. Now use whatever ingredients you like between the layers of eggplant.

Scatter the mozzarella, mushrooms, and/or the meatballs, spoon on a coating of marinara sauce and some of the romano. Cover with a layer of eggplant and then do this again and cover with more eggplant. Spoon sauce over top with more grated romano over that. Go a little easy on the sauce. If the dish is too soupy the layers will not hold together firmly. Bake at 350 for about 30-40 minutes or until it is heated through and bubbling around the edges.

Let the finished dish cool and settle for about 15 minutes before slicing. The layers might slide apart if you serve it right out of the oven. Place a gravy boat at the table with extra sauce.

Batter Fried Vegetables

You might see this dish listed on menus as Fritto Misto. It can be made up of any combination of vegetables but the crunchier ones are best.

You Will Need:

3 small zucchini, unpeeled and cut into spears about 2½"

1 small cauliflower, broken into florets about ¾" in diameter

1 bunch of broccoli, broken into florets about ¾" in diameter

For the Batter:

2 large eggs

1½ tablespoons olive oil

⅔ cup water

½ teaspoon salt

¾ cup flour

Canola oil for frying

Combine the flour and salt. Beat the eggs a bit and add the water and oil. Add the liquid ingredients to the flour mixture, whisking in a third of them at a time. Make the batter an hour or more ahead of use so that it becomes homogenized. It should be not quite like a pancake batter, just thick enough to cling to the vegetables.

While the batter is standing, prepare your veggies. If you want the cauliflower to be a bit more tender, steam the florets for a few minutes, take them off the heat and plunge them into an ice bath. Drain and use.

Using a deep pot, heat about 2 ½" of canola oil to medium high. You can check the readiness by testing a small piece of batter coated vegetable. If it rises to the top and begins to turn golden, the oil is ready. If it turns brown, it is too hot. Dip the vegetables in the batter and drop carefully into the hot oil. Turn them as they fry to a golden brown. Drain on paper towels. Keep warm at the back of the stove loosely covered with foil while you continue to prepare the rest of the vegetables. Don't do them too far ahead of time—they can soften in the oven. Coarsely grate Parmesan over the top for serving.

Sauteed Spinach

Note:

If you have a splatter lid for your skillet, it would come in handy for this recipe. It will allow the steam to escape and also will minimize the stovetop mess from the spray.

Fresh spinach is especially tender in the spring and early summer when you can get beautiful bunches of it from the local farmers. You can see that certain varieties have larger leaves and they are more coarse as the season progresses. If you buy the spinach in sealed packages that say Washed and Ready to Use I would still rinse it right before cooking and shake as much water off of it as possible. I am a bit wary of products that make it through the marketing process for such a long period of time so I only buy it when the fresh stuff doesn't look good.

If you are using the bagged leaves, eight ounces will provide 2-3 generous side dish servings. If you are buying bunches, two will be plenty and will allow for the trimming of the stems and any tough leaves. Leftovers can always be used in a quiche or omelet.

You Will Need:

8 ounces or 1-2 bunches of tender spinach, stems removed

Olive oil to coat your skillet

2-3 peeled and smashed garlic cloves

½ lemon

Coarse salt and fresh ground pepper to taste

If you are using bunches of spinach, trim them and place in cold water to cover in a very large bowl. Toss the leaves around a bit and then remove them to a colander. Do this three times or until you do not see any dirt or sand in the water. If you are using the bagged leaves, just rinse them once. Toss them in the colander until most of the water is off of them. In a large skillet, heat oil and garlic on medium high, turning the cloves until they are golden, not brown. Remove them from the oil and save.

Pile spinach leaves in skillet – they will mound up pretty high. They will immediately begin to sizzle and you will need to start turning them quickly with tongs. Keep cooking and turning until the spinach is somewhat limp and a bit darkened. This happens in just a few minutes. Remove from heat and toss in the saved garlic (you can chop it a bit if you like). You can keep this on the back of the stovetop while the rest of your dinner is cooking. It does not need to be hot—warm is fine. Arrange on a serving plate, sprinkle with salt and pepper and squeeze the lemon over the top.

Easy Do-Ahead Mashed Potatoes

You Will Need:

3 pounds potatoes, peeled and cubed

8 ounces cream cheese or ½ sour cream and ½ cream cheese

2 eggs

2 tablespoons flour

1 tablespoon minced fresh parsley

1 tablespoon minced chives

salt and pepper to taste

Boil potatoes until tender. Drain well and place in large mixer bowl along with cream cheese. The cream cheese will soften if you put it in the bottom of the bowl and then add the hot potatoes on top. Beat for a few minutes to break up the potatoes then add the eggs and flour and beat until smooth but not paste-like. Stir in chopped parsley and chives and also salt and pepper to your liking. Turn into a buttered shallow baking pan and bake, uncovered, at 325 for 30 minutes.

This can be prepared and refrigerated the day before and brought to room temperature before baking.

Note:

I use red potatoes, but there are many good varieties out there these days for you to try. Yukon Gold are good and, if you have russets they will work, although they are sometimes a bit mealy.

Twice Baked Potatoes

Note:

This is a great recipe for stocking your freezer with a very delicious and easy to use side dish for everyday meals or a company dinner. It's also a good way to use small bits of cheese that may be hanging out in the refrigerator.

You can make these a bit ahead and, when ready to use, bake them for about 20-30 minutes in a 375 degree oven.

If you want to make the potatoes up to a month ahead, fill the shells, place them on a waxed paper lined cookie sheet and freeze until hard. At this point immediately put them in zip bags for storing. When ready to use, thaw however many you need almost completely and continue with the second baking. You may have to bake them 5-10 minutes longer if they are still a bit cold.

You Will Need:

4 large baking potatoes

4 tablespoons butter

4 ounces cream cheese

Grated cheese (cheddar, Parmesan, brie, whatever you choose)

1½ tablespoons minced parsley

Salt and pepper to taste

Half and half, enough to whip into potatoes

Sour cream, optional

First, choose baking potatoes that are all about the same size. I use large but not huge ones or you could use medium sized ones, too, especially if you are making them for kids. Scrub the potatoes very well with an abrasive sponge or stiff brush. Cut a few slits along the sides where you will be cutting the potatoes in half

Potatoes bake well in a 400 oven but I have done them at 375 if I am cooking something that requires the oven to be used at the same time. Place the potatoes on the rack on a sheet of foil but do not wrap them. This keeps the skins crisp. Depending on the temperature and size of the potatoes they will take anywhere from 45 minutes to over an hour. Test them by squeezing them just a little to see if they are soft.

Remove from oven and let cool just until you can handle them. While the potatoes are cooling see what you have to add to them.

Cut each potato in half lengthwise. In a large mixer bowl, drop ½ stick of butter and 4 ounces of cream cheese. Scoop the insides out of the potatoes onto these ingredients. The heat from the potatoes will soften the butter and cream cheese. Mix on low for a minute or two and then on medium until combined. Do not overmix or they will turn out soupy. Add grated cheese and the parsley and continue mixing, adding a little half and half if you need to thin the mixture. Do not use too much because you want the mixture to be stiff enough that you can pull up little peaks on top.

Potato Pancakes

Practice this for breakfast sometime using one large potato. You will easily get the hang of it and if not, you will know what adjustments to make.

You Will Need;

1 large potato for every two people

Canola oil to coat skillet to ¼ inch

Sea salt and pepper, to taste

Peel the potato – russets work well for this—and, using the large holes on a box grater, shred it onto the center of a smooth cotton dish towel. An old one will do nicely because it is probably threadbare enough to let moisture seep through. Bring the long sides over the potatoes and, twisting each end of the towel in opposite directions, tighten it until the moisture is dripping from the towel.

Using enough oil to coat the bottom of a large skillet, heat on medium high. Grasp enough of the potatoes to make the size servings you want. Drop them into the skillet and then turn down the heat to medium.

Tongs work well for this. Flatten each pile a bit and sprinkle with salt and pepper. When the bottom side turns golden brown, flip to the other side. It may take about five minutes on each side, so adjust your heat accordingly. You want the potatoes to be done and the outside to be crunchy.

If you are making a lot of these, remove the finished pancakes onto a rack that is set on a cookie sheet. Keep warm in a 200 degree oven.

Note:

Russets are good for this because they cook quickly and are a fairly dry potato. You can always try other varieties that you like.

Home Fries

Note:

If you would like, you can heat up some sautéed onions (recipe follows) towards the end of cooking. Make a bed of the onions and heap the potatoes on top. Scatter with chopped parsley for a prettier presentation.

I actually have to chase the kids away when I am cooking these or we wouldn't end up with enough to serve at dinner. They absolutely love them. I use red potatoes but Yukon Gold or new white ones will do. Russets fall apart too easily – perfect for other things but not for these fries. Picture how many chunks you can get out of a potato and buy what you need for your family or guests.

You Will Need:

Potatoes, peeled or unpeeled

Canola oil

Sea salt

Freshly ground pepper

Scrub the potatoes well or peel them if you don't want the skins on. I prefer unpeeled red potatoes. Cut them in chunks of about ¾" and place them in a pot and cover with cold water an inch above the potatoes. Bring to a gentle boil and cook until they are still firm but almost done. Remove from heat and drain. You can do this early in the day or even the night before. Refrigerate if you are keeping them overnight.

For the next step, you will be browning the potatoes in about ¼" of oil in a skillet that is roomy enough to hold one layer of them. Set the heat at medium high, testing one piece of potato for perfect temperature. If it darkens too quickly, turn down the heat a little. You want them to be golden brown on all sides so turn them as they cook. Tongs work well for turning. Remove with a slotted spoon when they are done and lay out on paper towels to remove any oil that may still be clinging to them. Keep them warm in the oven at 200 degrees while you are cooking the rest.

Sauteed Onions

This is a very slow cooking recipe so I like to prepare it when I am in the kitchen doing other things. I listen to the radio and give the onions an occasional toss in between emptying the dishwasher or tidying up a shelf or two. These are always a great topping for a steak or hamburger.

You Will Need:

2 medium to large yellow or white onions

3 tablespoons olive oil

3 tablespoon unsalted butter

2 tablespoons sugar

Cut about ½" from the top of the onion and peel away the outer layer. Leave the root end on so that it will hold the onion together. Slice the onion into ¼" rings or whatever thickness you would like. Heat the oil and butter in a 10 or 12 inch skillet over medium low heat. Separate the rings and lay them around in the skillet. Using your tongs, toss them around as they cook. When they are a bit soft, sprinkle them with the sugar and toss them. Keep cooking as the sugar helps them to caramelize. Be sure you are keeping the heat low enough that they don't burn and adjust your stove accordingly. You are the one who knows how your stove operates so just keep that slow cooking going until they are golden.

Note:

If you are preparing the onions early in the day of your dinner they will be fine at room temperature. Refrigerated, they will keep well for 4–5 days.

If I am fixing a steak or hamburger for the same meal, I remove the onions to a heatproof dish and add a bit of oil to the skillet so that I can add flavor to the meat while it is cooking.

Baked Onions with Thyme

This is a deliciously sweet and very pretty dish for company. The edges of the cooked onions become tipped with a deep red color like roses in full bloom. Arrange them around a perfectly roasted cut of beef and you will have a dynamite presentation. The recipe will yield twelve although you can easily adjust the amounts to suit your needs.

You Will Need:

6 large red onions (about 2½" in diameter)

3 tablespoons olive oil

10 sprigs fresh thyme or a few teaspoons dried

Salt and pepper to taste

½ cup dry red wine

¼ cup water

Cut off the ends of the onions and then cut them in half crosswise. Discard outer layer of onion and arrange them, trimmed ends down in an oiled baking pan. Drizzle with the olive oil and season with salt and pepper. Scatter the thyme on top and pour wine gently over onions.

Bake for 30-40 minutes uncovered in a 400 oven, basting a few times with the pan juices. Add water to pan and bake until lightly browned and tender, about 50 minutes more. Check once in a while to make sure the pan is not drying out. Add some water if it is.

Serve hot or at room temperature.

Port Wine Salad Dressing Over Mesclun Mix & Fresh Figs

This salad dressing is delicious and sweet – boiling it down does that. I use a good port wine but not the most expensive. The range of prices is very wide – somewhere in the middle works for me.

You Will Need:

1 cup ruby port wine

1 tablespoon sugar

¼ cup balsamic vinegar

¾ cup olive oil

Mesclun greens

2 fresh figs per serving, halved lengthwise

2 tablespoons crumbled gorgonzola or bleu cheese per serving

6 walnut halves per serving, toasted

First, on a cookie sheet, toast walnuts in a 350 degree oven for 10 minutes or just until lightly brown. Shake them a few times while they are in the oven and watch carefully. They can go from brown to burnt very quickly. Set aside.

Measure wine into a small saucepan and heat on medium high until reduced to ½ cup. Add sugar and stir to dissolve. Remove from heat and add ¼ cup balsamic vinegar, then whisk in ¾ cup olive oil. Keep a bit warm on the back of the stove.

Place individual servings of mesclun greens on salad plates, garnish with fig halves, crumbled gorgonzola and toasted walnuts.

Note:

When figs are not in season, sliced crisp pears are a good substitute. Dried chopped apricots or cranberries can work too. Do not overdress the salad—in fact, never overdress any salad. It's better to add a bit more later than to have soggy greens.

Strawberry Spinach Salad

Note:

The dressing keeps well in the refrigerator. It can be used with other salads or is nice lightly drizzled over fruit.

All you need for this simple and delicious salad is a bowl full of spinach and sliced strawberries. The dressing can be made days ahead of time and is ample enough for a larger salad or for use at a later time.

You Will Need:

Spinach leaves, torn

Strawberries, sliced

For the dressing:

1 cup sugar

3 tablespoons poppy seeds

3 tablespoons sesame seeds

½ cup minced mild onion

1 teaspoon Worcestershire

½ teaspoon paprika

½ cup cider vinegar

1 cup oil

Mix the dressing ingredients together in a food processor, a blender or a glass jar that has a tight lid. Be sure that it is very well combined. Shortly before serving, pour just enough of the dressing over the spinach and strawberries and toss. Remember, don't overdress it – soggy isn't good.

Vegetable Rice Salad

If you want something that is the hit of the pot luck, try this recipe. It makes around 10 cups but you can adjust the recipe to make less.

You Will Need:

1½ cups dry rice (I use basmati)

2½ cups water

1 bunch thinly sliced green onions, white and part of green

1 minced shallot

½ large red pepper, thin slices or dice

½ large green pepper, thin slices or dice

½ cup dried currants

1 cup frozen green peas, blanched

½ cup sliced black olives

½ cup toasted slivered almonds

2 tablespoons dried dill

2 tablespoons minced parsley or 1 tablespoon dried

Salt and pepper to taste

Vinaigrette (recipe follows)

Cook rice in the usual manner and when it is cooked and still hot empty it into a large bowl. Lightly toss it around a bit and add enough of the vinaigrette to coat it. Cool to room temperature.

Add remaining ingredients, toss and then add more vinaigrette as needed. You do not want it to be swimming in the dressing, just coated nicely.

Note:

This is good served at room temperature but you can make it ahead, store it in the refrigerator and then bring it back to room temp for serving. The type of rice I use cooks perfectly with the amount of water in this recipe. You may find that the one you buy needs a different proportion so be sure to check the instructions before cooking.

You can use a good bottled Italian dressing if you are pressed for time. Also, as a do-ahead, try chopping all of your vegetables the night before so that you can quickly combine them with the rice the next day.

Vinaigrette

You Will Need:

2 tablespoons Dijon mustard

½ cup red wine vinegar

2 teaspoons sugar

½ teaspoon each salt and pepper or to taste

1 cup extra virgin olive oil

Whisk together 1 tablespoon Dijon Mustard, ¼ cup red wine vinegar, 1 teaspoon sugar, ½ teaspoon of salt and pepper. Continue to whisk while slowly adding 1 cup olive oil. You can also use a food processor to mix or just shake up the ingredients in a glass jar adding ¼ of the olive oil at a time.

Ever Ready Salad Dressing

I make this dressing just about every week. It is very easy and keeps well without refrigeration. I make a cup of it because we have a small salad with dinner almost every night. You can decide how much you will use within a week and measure your ingredients accordingly. I recommend a cold pressed extra virgin olive oil. The balsamic vinegar that is from Modena is regulated by law and is labeled according to the number of years that is has aged. The older it is the more intense it is and, sad to say, the more expensive too.

You Will Need:

3 parts extra virgin olive oil

1 part balsamic vinegar

1 generous teaspoon of a sweetener – sugar, honey, raspberry jam or your choice for every half cup of dressing

Herbs if you like

Measure your ingredients into a pint jar with a tight lid. Shake it well, making sure that all of the components are totally blended.

It is important that you not overdress your green salad. It will become a soggy mess. For two people you could start with 1–2 tablespoons and toss it around. It should be very lightly coated.

I buy mesclun greens and, in the winter, use dried or fresh fruit, nuts and blue cheese over top. In the summer, when the tomatoes are finally tasty there is nothing better than a tomato, cucumber and red onion salad with toasted bread cubes. Recipe follows for making your own croutons.

Croutons

Instead of tossing out your somewhat stale half loaf of bread try making these very simple croutons to use with salads, soup or whatever. You can personalize them by using the herbs that you prefer and your kitchen will smell yummy while they're baking. They are so much better than the store bought ones that my whole family eats them like popcorn. Sometimes I hide them and I'm not saying where!

You Will Need:

6 thick slices of coarse slightly stale bread

2 tablespoons melted butter

2 tablespoons olive oil

Herbs of your choice (thyme, parsley, sage, whatever), minced

Salt and pepper to taste

Remove most of the crust from bread and cut it into cubes that are almost ¾" on each side. Scatter them on a large ungreased baking sheet. Combine the butter and oil in a small bowl and whisk to blend. Drizzle this over the bread cubes and toss them around so that the butter and oil are evenly distributed. Sprinkle the herbs on top, toss the bread cubes again and sprinkle a bit with the salt and pepper. Bake for about 45 minutes at 300, shaking the pan occasionally and checking for even browning. You will want them to be a nice golden color.

Note:

The croutons will keep well for a week or so. A brown bag with waxed paper on the bottom is fine for storing them.

Very Good Coleslaw

I like to use both the green and red cabbage for this so that, when combined with a carrot or two, it is a very colorful salad.

You Will Need:

4 cups shredded cabbage, half red and half green

1 cup shredded carrot

½ cup top quality mayo

3 tablespoons sour cream, regular or low fat

1 tablespoon sugar

1 tablespoon white vinegar

1 teaspoon dry mustard

1 teaspoon celery salt, optional

Salt and pepper to taste

Decide how coarsely shredded you would like your vegetables and use the appropriate blade in your food processor. In a large bowl, toss them to combine.

In a medium bowl, whisk the mayo and the other ingredients until well mixed. If you are choosing to use celery salt, keep this in mind when deciding how much additional salt to use.

An hour or more before serving add enough of the dressing to coat the veggies without having them swimming in it. It's one of those "less is more" things because the salad actually tastes fresher and crispier that way.

Note:

The leftovers are good the next day but I recommend making the salad on the morning of the dinner party.

Soups & Sauces

TURTLE SOUP

Although I have no recipe for turtle soup in this book I am slipping in this story about my Italian grandfather and his custom of trapping a snapping turtle and turning it into soup. I love turtles so the tradition makes me cringe but grandpa held on to the old ways as he and my grandmother struggled to feed their family of seven children, two boarders, a daughter-in-law and granddaughter and an occasional extra person at the table.

There were many years and quite a few turtles in my grandfather's life and in 1957 I saw, close up, the last one that he caught. Grandpa was seventy two years old by then and had, for many years, participated in an annual fishing trip to Ontario, Canada. It was a day long trip, each September, to Toronto from Steubenville, Ohio and from there another 100 miles Northeast to the area of the Trent River. The destination was the Bonavista Camp, near the towns of Frankford and Stirling, where $7.00 a day would buy you lodging, breakfast, dinner and two snacks, all you could eat.

The fishing party usually included Grandpa, his son Joe, and Joe's friends from the mill, Shorty and Paul. The mission was to collect, in a week, several large coolers of fish and, for Grandpa, the biggest snapping turtle he could trap. I'm not sure what types of fish were caught and I don't know anything about how to trap a turtle, but some years Grandpa was successful and he would return to Steubenville with his catch, butcher it and then make and preserve quarts of turtle soup.

In 1957 Grandpa returned home once more with a live, though restrained, snapping turtle which, under normal circumstances, he would keep in the cellar until sometime in the next week when it would meet its sad end. Until then the turtle was supposed to hang out in a large washtub that sat on the dirt floor of the big room at the bottom of the stairs but the tub was not much bigger than the turtle and he could tip it over and easily walk out and about. Two smaller rooms, one containing the press and wooden barrels for Grandpa's winemaking and the other, a pantry filled with dusty glass jars, were not accessible to him because of the few steps that led up to them.

The turtle shared his territory with a washing machine and a clothesline. Uncle Joe, his wife Helen and their two boys lived with Grandpa, and one of Aunt Helen's tasks was to do the laundry and hang the clothes on the line, outside in sunshine or in the cellar on rainy days. The laundry was mounting and so was Aunt Helen's terror. She would not go downstairs because, like all of us, she had heard stories of snapping turtles and how their jaws could sever a person's arm or leg. We were convinced that Grandpa's turtle, benign as it looked, could do just that.

As a kid, I found this part of Grandpa's life much more interesting than his work in the steel mill and even his ever present gardening. As I stood on the cellar steps, secure in the knowledge that turtles couldn't climb stairs, I was in awe of this creature. It was an opportunity to view nature since we didn't go to zoos or see any other type of non-domesticated animal.

Though everyone had come to expect the arrival of the turtle, this was, in fact, the last one to dwell in Grandpa's cellar and, sadly, Grandpa's last fishing trip. Looking back on it, I'm not sure if he was stalling or just losing track of the sequence of events. The turtle was not butchered and it roamed around on the dirt floor for several weeks. It seemed that Grandpa had no intention of turning it into soup.

Aunt Helen was growing desperate and was talking to the sisters-in-law and begging for a solution to this dilemma. It was a discussion involving the women of the family, since the men, off to work, thought that Grandpa would eventually shift into cooking gear. No one wanted to anger him because, even though he was only about 5'4" and didn't talk much, he was still the patriarch of the family and had command of his own house and his own turtle.

October arrived, the weather was beginning to turn cold and Grandpa got busy closing down his garden, a time consuming job since the garden filled the entire yard. There were next year's seeds to be prepared from the tomatoes and peppers, the fig tree to be wrapped and old plants to be cut down and mulched. The wine grapes had to be harvested and pressed and readied for the barrels. After his chores were done, it was assumed that he would turn to the business of making soup. But when he finished his outdoor work and, as it was getting colder and no one would be using the yard, he set the turtle loose there. It followed its instincts and dug itself into the still soft ground and settled in for the winter.

Most everyone, even Grandpa, seemed to forget about the whole thing but then came spring and along with it the old turtle, which emerged from the softening ground for a walk around the bare back yard. The family had to take a stand. Though Grandpa was still technically the boss, the turtle had to go.

There was no sentimentality attached to the turtle's end. My cousin, the one who lived there, told me about it. The turtle was offered some food and when his head popped out someone hit him a hard blow with an axe. His shell was ripped off and the carcass was pinned to the clothesline to bleed out.

I prefer to envision a fairy tale ending in which Grandpa and the turtle are walking to the steel mill with its chimneys belching smoke and soot, the mill where Grandpa had spent most every day of his life.

CHICKEN COOP

It's nice to have some of the chicken farmers looking out for us these days with organic, free range, low fat, no hormone birds. I appreciate it but I wouldn't mind visiting once again the chicken store near Mr. Lascaro's house. I think I was about six years old when I went there with my mother.

There were big birds, one to a cage, all along the walls of the long narrow building and, as I recall, it was kind of smelly in there with much clucking and squawking that got louder as we entered. My mother spoke to Mr. Lascaro in Italian and then he opened one of the cages, pulled out a chicken and walked out the back door with it. He returned soon with a nicely wrapped package for us.

It was a time when little kids weren't part of the conversations or offered explanations and I'm glad I didn't know anything because I really liked those chickens. I still like chickens and I love to sit in the sun in the Bolls' backyard and watch their chickens strut their stuff.

Chicken Soup

You will need:

1 whole chicken or 3 pounds of necks and backs with a few thighs

6 carrots cut in chunks

3 celery stalks

1 large onion, peeled and cut into fourths

2 or 3 bay leaves

2 large eggs, beaten

3 tablespoons finely grated Parmesan or Romano

3 tablespoons finely chopped parsley

Salt and pepper to taste

Cooked rice or noodles

In a very large pot, place chicken, whole or parts, and cover it with 2-3 inches of cold water above the chicken. Bring this to a boil and leave it at a soft boil as the scum rises to the top. Spoon this off and then add the carrots, celery, onion and bay leaves to the pot. Bring back to a boil and then reduce heat so that it is just simmering. Continue this slow cooking with the lid partly on for about two hours. The meat should be falling off the bones by then. Let cool slightly and ladle the broth through a sieve into a large bowl. Retrieve the carrots and the chicken from the sieve and toss the other things out. Remove the meat from the bones and save this separately.

At this point you can separate some of the meat and carrots to use in a pot pie, and use the smaller bits for the soup. Cut the carrots for the pot pie into slices, saving a few to mash up for the soup.

Refrigerate the broth overnight and the fat will harden on the top. Remove the fat—it has already imparted its flavor to the broth so don't worry that you are discarding it. If you are planning to make the pot pie later in the week refrigerate two cups of the broth for that.

Before assembling the soup, cook a cup of rice or 4 ounces of pasta and set aside. I use basmati rice because I like it but you may have a variety that you prefer. No instant rice, please. If you are using pasta, choose

Note:

Since you are probably buying your chicken at the market you may have noticed that the breast meat is usually very lean and that there is also very little fat on the rest of the bird. Keeping your diet lean is a good thing but it is the fat that lends flavor to your broth. To compensate for this, if you are making soup, ask the butcher for necks and backs. They are inexpensive and nowadays are frozen in large packages. Add to these a few thighs and maybe a piece of breast if you are going to need chunks of meat for a pot pie or hearty soup. When you refrigerate the broth most of the fat will rise to the top and harden and it can be skimmed off. The soup will retain the flavor and still have a lower fat content.

You can do many variations on the soups that you use this broth for and it is also perfect for the pot pie recipe in this book.

Note:

I prefer to ladle the soup into the individual bowls and then add some of the rice (or the pasta) to the bowl. This way you can store the leftover broth and the left-over rice or noodles separately and then reheat the broth without overcooking the rice or pasta.

Recently my friend Mariann, who is as thrifty as I am, told me that she adds the end of the Parmesan – the part with the rind – to the broth as it is cooking. It can be discarded after it imparts its last bit of flavor to the soup.

the ones you like. I like shells or broken up wide noodles but, again, it is up to you.

For the soup, smash the cooked carrots with a fork and add that and the smaller chunks of chicken to the pot. Bring the heat back up to a slow simmer.

In a small bowl, beat the eggs with 2 tablespoons finely grated Parmesan or Romano. Add a little of the hot broth gradually to the egg mixture, beating while adding it. Then add this back to the pot, stirring it in to incorporate. Add parsley and salt and pepper to taste.

If your broth is not as flavorful as you would expect you can add a few teaspoons of a product called Better than Bouillon. It is organic and low sodium – an excellent product.

ITALIAN WEDDING SOUP

Well, here we are at our wedding reception, a happy couple to be sure, happy to have family and friends to share in our wonderful Italian celebration. We were actually smiling because we had surmounted the obstacles to our getting married – I was Catholic and Bucky was Presbyterian and, maybe more importantly, I am Italian and he is a real "Leave it to Beaver" American. This was the 1960's and my community, school and church were all Italian. I did and still do say that I am Italian.

Although it was difficult then, I see it as funny now, that nothing was too personal for some of my family's long time friends who would ask me, among other things, if Bucky was the boy my mother was upset about (he was) and is he a nice boy (he is) and did I know that someday he might look down on me for being an Italian (he wouldn't). They just came right out with it but they came to love him almost as much as I did.

When our big day finally arrived it began with a long, long High Mass and wedding ceremony presided over by two priests and a Monsignor. How patient all of Bucky's family and guests were! Most of them were not Catholic. They deserved a party and later in the day they got one.

It began with a cocktail hour and then a complete Italian dinner starting with a small antipasto plate followed by a serving of wedding soup. Next came the pasta course and salad, after which the American guests, thinking the dinner was over, began to get up just as the servers were bringing in the meat and vegetables. The wine was flowing and the glasses were being tapped constantly for the bride and groom to kiss.

I have been to many Italian weddings over the years, even when I was a kid and didn't want to go. Often I was a flower girl. I remember that the old folks did impromptu Italian singing with the band and they danced the tarantella and I may have rolled my eyes over it too much. They did it at our wedding and for some reason I loved it.

Wedding Soup became a tradition at Italian weddings in this country, especially among the immigrants who had settled in western Pennsylvania and the adjacent towns of eastern Ohio. In fact, its Italian name is "minestra maritata", so named for the fact that the meat and the vegetables were married (combined in a relationship) during the cooking. It's a wonderful and beautiful dish. Wedding or not, I hope you will try it.

Italian Wedding Soup

You Will Need:

6 cups chicken broth

½ pound ground beef or pork or a mix of both

Olive oil, enough to coat a large enough skillet to hold the meatballs

1 bunch of spinach, kale or escarole, coarsely chopped

2 eggs

¼ cup grated Parmesan

Salt and pepper

1 cup orzo

First, using just the pork and beef, form very small meatballs about the size of a grape, making sure they are tight enough to hold together. Place the meatballs in a skillet coated with olive oil and move them around while they are browning. They will cook more in the soup so don't overcook them.

In a medium bowl beat the two eggs with the grated cheese and set aside.

Boil the orzo until almost cooked. Drain and set aside.

Heat the broth in a large pot on high and then turn it down to a simmer. Add the meatballs and cook gently for a few minutes. Add ¼ cup of the broth to the beaten egg mixture, whisking to keep the eggs from cooking. Return mixture to the pot while stirring.

Add the greens and the orzo a few minutes before serving. Taste for salt and pepper. Serve in soup plates.

Note:

This soup should not be thick. Use only enough of the greens and orzo so that the broth is the major part of the soup. It looks very pretty that way.

Pasta e Fagioli

My Dad (he's the one on the right) was the oldest of seven children and the first in his family to go away to college. He and some of his Italian pals worked in the steel mills and elsewhere in the summer and, with their earnings and some help from family and friends, they went off every fall to study at Ohio State University. They lived together in a big rented house and survived on pots of soup and pasta with sugo (sauce) to make ends meet. Eventually they came home as doctors, dentists, attorneys, accountants and teachers and they became a moving force in the town in which they grew up as the children of immigrants.

This was my father's favorite soup and, with its combination of protein, vegetables, and pasta you will find that it is a very healthful dish for your family. And a pretty thrifty one, too!

Before the introduction of the food processor, the paste (or battuto) to start this soup was made by laying out the pieces of salt pork, topping them with the garlic, celery leaves and onion and pounding them with the thick edge of a chef's knife. The pounding and turning over and pounding again and turning produces an almost spreadable product. This takes about 15 minutes. The food processor takes a few minutes so, if you have one, use it.

Fagioli are beans such as kidney or pinto or cannellini and using the canned beans works out fine. You can find salt pork in most markets or you can use a few slicess of pancetta which is a type of Italian bacon.

You Will Need:

4 thick slices of lean salt pork or pancetta

3 large cloves of garlic

Leafy tops of celery

¼ large onion, chopped

1 chopped carrot, optional

4 tablespoons olive oil

1 quart water

32 ounce can crushed tomatoes

Note:

I recommend cooking the pasta separately, and then adding some to each person's bowl. This works well and keeps the pasta from overcooking in the pot.

2 tablespoons tomato paste

3 cups kidney or other beans

2 cups small pasta, cooked al dente

⅓ cup minced fresh parsley

Parmesan or Romano for grating

Chop the slices of the salt pork and drop them into the bowl of your food processor along with the garlic, the celery and onion. Add 2 tablespoons of olive oil and a carrot if you like. Process until it is almost a paste. Saute this in 2 tablespoons of olive oil in a large pot.

Add the water, crushed tomatoes, tomato paste and salt to taste. Bring to a boil and then simmer for about 15 minutes and add about 3 cups of beans. Simmer for another 10-15 minutes.

There are several options on the pasta—tubettini, elbows or something of that size. Don't use the really small ones like orzo. While the soup is simmering, bring another pot of water to a boil and add your pasta. Cook to al dente, drain, and then add at the very last few minutes to the soup. If you prefer to cook it in the soup broth you will need more water in the broth as some will be absorbed into the pasta.

Right before serving add fresh parsley.

Serve the soup in pasta bowls with a generous shaving of Parmesan or just have your guests add their own at the table.

Sausage Spinach Soup

This tasty soup is very good for a last minute company or family dinner.

You Will Need:

1 pound ground sausage, mild or medium

Olive oil

3-4 cloves garlic, finely chopped

1 29 ounce can chopped tomatoes

4 cups chicken broth

8 ounces cooked pasta, mini bowties or other small variety

1 large bunch fresh spinach, washed, stemmed and roughly chopped

Grated Parmesan or Romano (optional)

Coat the bottom of a large pot with olive oil and heat to a bit above medium. Add the sausage and break it up with a spatula as it is cooking. When the sausage has almost lost its pink color pour off any grease that has accumulated. Add the garlic and continue cooking and stirring until the garlic is softened. Add chopped tomatoes and chicken broth. Bring soup back to a simmer.

While this is cooking, fill another large pot with water and bring to boil. Add a few tablespoons of salt and cook the pasta following the directions on the package. Do not cook beyond the al dente stage. Drain the pasta, return it to the pot and add a bit of olive oil to keep it from clumping together. Set aside.

Right before serving add the spinach to the soup pot and cook just until it is wilted. To serve, place some of the pasta in each bowl (start with ¼ cup) and ladle the hot soup over it. If desired, top with coarsely grated Parmesan or Romano.

Note:

Again, I like to cook the pasta separately because if the soup is staying warm on the stove the pasta will continue to cook and become way too soft. I do this with rice that is added to the soup also and I think you will find that it works well.

Winter Vegetable Soup

During the winter months when the choice of other vegetables is limited, you can almost always find lovely leeks, onions and spinach. This is a very flavorful and simple soup that will warm you up on a cold day.

You Will Need:

4 slices bacon or salt pork, cut into 1" pieces

4 tablespoons butter

2 cups chopped leeks

1 cup chopped onions

1 cup diced celery, including some leaves

1 teaspoon dried tarragon

1 teaspoon dried thyme

5 cups chicken broth, homemade or a good brand like Pacific Organic

2½ cups diced red potatoes, skins on

1 pound spinach leaves, coarsely chopped

Salt and pepper to taste

¾ cup heavy cream

To prepare the leeks, cut off the root end and trim the tops to about an inch and a half above the white part. Pull the leeks apart and submerge them in a bowl of cold water. Swish them around to remove the dirt that has collected between the layers, pour off the water and do this two more times or until the water is clear. Leeks can be very sandy so be sure they are clean. Do this to the spinach leaves also as they are sometimes pretty dirty. If you buy the pre-washed spinach, you should still rinse them just once.

In a large pot, cook the bacon or salt pork over low heat until the fat is rendered. If using bacon you can remove it with a slotted spoon and save the cooked pieces for an omelet or baked potato or over a spinach salad. If using the salt pork, remove the pieces and just throw them away.

Add the butter to the pot and, when it is melted, add the onions, leeks and celery. Cook over medium low heat until wilted but not browned—about 10-15 minutes. Season with thyme and tarragon. Add the chicken broth and the potatoes and turn the heat up to simmer. Cook until the potatoes are tender but not mushy. Add half of the spinach and cook for one minute.

Remove soup from the heat and puree half of it in a food processor. Return it to the pot. At this time, taste for salt and pepper and adjust according to what you would like. Place pot over low heat and add the remaining spinach and the cream. Heat through but do not boil.

Potato Soup

NOTE:

If you like a lot of bacon (and who doesn't) you can adjust the recipe as you desire. You could also add canned clams to make it into a quick chowder.

At our house, if it's your birthday, you can choose the dinner menu and I will cook it. Bucky's is the most predictable because every year his selection is Potato Soup. The dessert is Apple Fritters, the recipe in this book. I add a green salad and something with more protein just to balance the whole thing out.

In truth I had never eaten a fritter myself but I happened to find a recipe in the newspaper which, after a few tries, I adjusted a bit. Bucky was very happy and the grandkids loved it too.

You Will Need:

5-6 medium potatoes, peeled and cubed; russets work well

4 slices cooked bacon cut into ½ inch pieces

½ large onion, diced

1 teaspoon dry mustard

2 teaspoons Worcestershire

2 tablespoons minced fresh parsley or 1 tablespoon dried

2 tablespoons butter

3 cups whole milk

Coarsely grated medium cheddar for topping.

Snipped chives

Sauté bacon with diced onion over medium low heat. Stir it a few times during cooking and do not let the onions get too brown. Remove from pan with a slotted spoon and drain on a paper towel.

Using a pot that will hold all of the ingredients cover the potatoes with water and boil until they are tender but not mushy. Drain and return to the pot. Mash lightly, leaving some small pieces in the mix. Add bacon and onion, dry mustard, Worcestershire, parsley and butter. Stir to combine.

Stir in the milk and heat to just under boiling.

Serve with some grated cheddar cheese and a sprinkling of chives

Seafood Stew

This is an excellent and beautiful recipe that makes enough for four very generous servings. I like to use mussels but clams work well if you prefer.

You Will Need:

1½ pounds true cod or other firm fish. See Note.

2 dozen medium size raw shrimp, shelled

3 minced garlic cloves

3 tablespoons olive oil

16 mussels or clams

⅔ cup white wine

2 medium onions, chopped

1 green pepper, cut into thin strips

1 yellow pepper, cut into thin strips

2 tablespoons olive oil

1½ tablespoons flour

2 tablespoons tomato paste

1 cup clam juice

1 cup chicken broth

3-4 cups canned chopped tomatoes

2 tablespoons minced parsley

½ teaspoon each basil and oregano

Dried red pepper, optional

First, mix the shrimp and cubed fish with 3 minced garlic cloves and 3 tablespoons olive oil. Also, prepare your mussels in advance by scrubbing them well and pulling or scraping off the beards (the hairy threads that protrude from the shell. Set aside these things while preparing stew).

Note:

If you have a good fish market, they may sell you a mixture of chunks of firm fish that they have trimmed off of larger fillets. The last ones I bought were a combination of salmon, halibut and cod. They were a bargain and very fresh and delicious.

If you prefer a meatless entrée, substitute vegetable broth for the chicken broth.

To Prepare Stew: In a large deep saucepan, sauté the onions and one green pepper and one yellow pepper, cut into strips, in 2 tablespoons olive oil. Cook and stir until softened and beginning to color. Stir in 1 ½ tablespoons flour and 2 tablespoons tomato paste and cook over medium heat for a few minutes. Add 1 cup clam juice and 1 cup chicken broth. Stir in 3-4 cups canned chopped tomatoes, ½ teaspoon each basil and oregano. You can add a little dried red pepper if you like. Let stew simmer for 10 minutes or so.

While it is cooking, combine mussels or clams in a saucepan with 2/3 cup white wine. Cover, bring to a boil and let steam about five minutes or until open. Discard any that do not open.

At this point add the shrimp and cubed fish to the stew and simmer for 5 minutes. Add mussels or clams with cooking liquid and a few tablespoons minced parsley. Add salt and pepper to taste.

Dish this up in large pasta bowls, making sure that everyone gets some of each type of seafood. A side dish of rice is good for adding to the broth if guests wish.

Creamy Onion Soup with Shrimp

This is a very rich soup and it is a bit on the sweet side. The caramelizing of the onions will do that. It may seem like it is complicated but it is very much the opposite. The hour or so that it takes mostly involves stirring it every once in a while.

You Will Need:

¼ cup olive oil

6 tablespoons unsalted butter

4 large (not huge) white or yellow onions, chopped

2 teaspoons sugar

2 cups bottled clam juice

¼ cup dry white wine

¼ cup marsala

3 tablespoons basmati rice, uncooked

1½ teaspoons dried thyme

Salt and pepper to taste

2 cups heavy cream

1 pound cooked small shrimp

Coarsely chopped flat leaf parsley

I would suggest using a pot or a deep skillet about 12" in diameter so that the onions can be browned nicely without being crowded. Heat the oil and butter over medium heat, add the onions to the skillet, turn the heat down a notch, and stir them frequently. You can sprinkle them with 2 teaspoons of sugar to help them brown and caramelize. At first they will weep and then, as the liquid dissipates, they will begin to turn color.

Now, while you are hanging around the kitchen so that you can stir onions, you can measure out everything else. After the onions are ready,

stir in the clam juice, wine, marsala, rice, thyme and salt and pepper. Bring the mixture to a boil, then turn down to a simmer and cook for 30 minutes, stirring occasionally.

Remove from heat and puree in a food processor. You may have to do this in several batches depending on how much you are making. Return the soup to the pot and add the 2 cups of heavy cream. Heat the soup until hot but not boiling.

To serve, drop ¼ cup of shrimp in each soup plate and ladle the hot soup on top. Garnish with chopped parsley.

Seafood & Meats

WESTWARD HO

Bucky and I were married for about a year when Piper Aircraft Corporation, the company he was working for as a district manager, transferred us to Vancouver, Washington. When we told my parents about it they thought we meant we were going to Washington D.C. and, in truth, I, being geographically impaired, didn't realize just how far away from home we would be. I was apprehensive, to be sure, about leaving with a new baby and stepping into a whole new life. Bucky, who was known as Jim in his working life, left for Vancouver first and then, after spending some time with my parents, Cristianne and I joined him a week later. He picked us up at Portland Airport and, as we drove away, he said "Look out the back window." I did and there was the magnificent sight of Mt. Hood – a perfect welcome. I am still in awe of that very spectacular mountain.

In 1966 we moved down to Eugene, Oregon, a beautiful college town located in the Willamette Valley, right between the mountains of the Coast Range and the Cascades. If we drove an hour westward we could stand on the shore of the Pacific Ocean, as far on dry land as possible from our former homes. And so on a sweltering August day in the high 90's in Eugene, we packed up baby, blankets and picnic lunch, and drove to the beach town of Florence. It was a perfect way to beat the heat and play in the sand and splash in the water. The lesson we learned about Oregon that day was that hot in Eugene does not necessarily mean hot at the Coast.

I think we may be the only people in Oregon who don't go camping, but this was as close as we came. We arranged our blankets behind a pile of driftwood and set out Cristianne's toys and, since it was sunny and we were protected from a cold wind, we stayed relatively warm. We played in the sand and ran up into the shallow water. Bucky decided to change into his swim trunks at a nearby restroom and he came running back to do a macho dive into the Pacific. I think he may have set a record for time in and out—a quick baptism for our new life.

We gradually learned that living on the West Coast was different in many ways—I could probably count hundreds. But, since this IS a cookbook, I will mention that one of my very favorite experiences was when Bucky's outdoorsman brother Alex, who was already living in the Northwest, showed up and introduced us to a freshly caught salmon, larger than any fish I had ever seen close up. He had gutted it and slathered the cavity with mayo topped with thin slices of lemon and onion and a sprinkling of salt and pepper and dill. It was wrapped in foil, placed on a hot grill for about half an hour and then turned to cook on the other side. With my first forkful I had the same reaction that I believe Americans must have at their first taste of an authentic Italian dinner. Molto incredibile!

A FISH STORY

The small town where I grew up was located on the banks of the heavily polluted Ohio River and it was filled, so they said, with fish, although I never saw one through the murky water. I heard about the catfish, how big and ugly they were and about the fact that few people dared eat them. It was the fifties and environmentalism had not entered into the national conversation, and especially had not penetrated this valley that was dotted by steel mills and other factories. If a good job was weighed against toxic runoff and air pollution, the job would win. In truth, it was a different time.

Since we were Catholics, we had fish for dinner every Friday and it came from the freezer section of the grocery store. It was usually breaded and baked halibut or snapper and was only a small step better than the lentil soup that was served with it. I dreaded these Friday meals and my Dad knew it. Luckily he sat right around the corner of the table from me and he helped me out by stealing a bite or two when my mother wasn't looking.

A few years ago, while I was at the market trying to decide on which fish for dinner, the man behind the counter said, "We got some really good catfish in today." I told him my Ohio story and said, "That's something I just don't eat." He said, "This comes from Mississippi and it's farm raised and is ranked as a best choice on the sustainability chart."

And so, it sounded like I could support the drive for healthy, abundant oceans while having a fabulous dinner. I couldn't turn that down and I really liked the guy's salesmanship.

I became a big fan of catfish and also of the man behind the counter. He has steered me to the best and freshest seafood and he gave me a little chart from Seafood Watch. There is a website that will allow you to print one out for yourself and I hope you will do it. It is www.seafoodwatch.org

Crunchy Catfish

The following is my recipe for catfish. It is simple and very good and I make it often. One pound will serve three people and 1½ pounds will give you four very generous portions.

You Will Need:

1 pound catfish fillets

½ cup buttermilk

¾ cup medium grind cornmeal

½ teaspoon paprika

½ cup canola oil

Salt and pepper to taste

If the fillets are large cut them in half crosswise and salt and pepper them. Combine the cornmeal and paprika on a flat surface and pour the buttermilk into a shallow bowl. Dip the fish pieces in buttermilk, making sure they are completely coated all around. Press each one into the cornmeal, coating both sides and the edges. At this point you can refrigerate them, loosely covered, until ready to cook. You can do this early in the day or a few hours before cooking.

To cook, heat the oil in a large skillet to medium high. Test the temperature of the oil by cutting off a tiny piece of the fish and dropping it into the skillet. If it darkens too quickly, turn the heat down. Carefully set fillets in the hot oil and cook them until golden on each side. This will only take 3-4 minutes. Turn them with a wide spatula with a sharp edge to keep the coating intact. Do not crowd the skillet and cook in several batches if necessary.

Remove the fish from the skillet and place it in a baking dish—again do not crowd. Bake in a 375 oven for 10-15 minutes depending on the thickness of the fillets. You can check for doneness by inserting a knife into the thickest part and spreading the fillet enough to see the flesh. If the center looks raw cook it for a few more minutes.

Note:

Serve with lemon wedges, seafood sauce or tartar sauce, whatever you prefer. You can use this technique with other fish fillets that are the same texture as catfish. Fixed this way, you can also make tasty catfish sandwiches on French rolls with just a few lettuce leaves, tomato slices and some mayo or Thousand Island dressing. Add some coleslaw and potato salad on the side for a delicious summer dinner.

Simple Salmon

We eat seafood frequently and we feel fortunate to have such a variety to choose from at our markets here. We've tried many different kinds but I think our favorite remains salmon. In 30-40 minutes you can prepare a healthful dinner for four of baked salmon, sautéed fresh spinach with garlic, basmati rice and maybe a tossed salad with vinegar and oil dressing. The fish itself only takes 3 minutes of your time and 15 minutes of cooking time.

You Will Need:

1½ pounds of salmon fillet

2 tablespoons butter

1 tablespoon olive oil

1 tablespoon dill weed or to taste

Coarse sea salt

Freshly ground pepper

In a baking pan place 2 tablespoons of butter and 1 tablespoon of olive oil. Turn your oven to 375 and place the pan in the oven during the preheating. The butter will melt with the oil in a few minutes. Remove the pan from the oven and whisk the oil and melted butter so that it is evenly distributed. Place the fillet flesh side down onto the pan to butter it and then turn it over so it is skin side down. Sprinkle with salt, pepper and dill.

The salmon will take about 15-20 minutes depending on the thickness of the fillet. Place it in the 375 oven and after 15 minutes test it by running a sharp knife lengthwise down the thickest part of the fish. Spread it a bit and you will see if it is cooked or still a bit raw. Don't let it overcook or it will be dry.

In the time the salmon is baking, you can prepare rice following the directions for the type you are using. And while the rice and salmon are cooking you can saute the spinach which is easily done in 3-4 minutes. It will stay warm enough on the back of the stove when it is done.

Remove the salmon from the oven and cut into serving sized pieces. Lift these off of the skin onto a serving platter or serve on individual plates.

Note:

The spinach recipe is in the Vegetable section of this book and some thoughts on cooking rice are also there.

If you are preparing a salad for this meal, you may want to use the Ever Ready Dressing recipe in the Salad section of this book.

Salmon in Puff Pastry

This is delicious and beautiful enough to serve at a brunch buffet or even as an appetizer. It is effortless to prepare, especially if you are using the frozen puff pastry. Homemade dough would produce a crispier and more layered shell but making it is time consuming. A recipe for that dough is easy to find in any general cookbook.

You Will Need:

2 sheets frozen or homemade puff pastry (about 18 ounces)

1 pound salmon fillet

10 green onions

2 packed cups baby spinach leaves,

1 tablespoon dill weed

1 teaspoon coarse sea salt

Pepper to taste

Juice from half of a large lemon

1 tablespoon cold butter

1 large egg beaten with 1 tablespoon water

If using the frozen pastry, remove it from the freezer 40 minutes before using. Each sheet will be folded into thirds. Carefully open each one after it has thawed a bit. If it cracks at the seam wet it with a very small amount of water and seal it.

While the dough is thawing, cut salmon into ½" chunks, shred spinach and thinly slice green onions, discarding about 3" of the tops. Combine these ingredients in a bowl with the dill, salt, lemon juice and a bit of pepper. Gently toss. Refrigerate until ready to use.

Roll the dough on a lightly floured board until it is about 10"x12". Arrange half of the salmon mixture on one 12" side of the pastry, stopping at the middle and leaving a ¾" margin on the sides and edge. Top with tiny bits of butter. Brush the egg wash along all of the edges and pull the unfilled side of the pastry over the top so that you have a rectangle that is about 5"x10". Cut three diagonal slits on top and brush egg wash over the whole package. Repeat process with the other pastry and place both on a lightly floured baking sheet.

Refrigerate for at least three hours. If you are going to bake them early in the morning they will be fine in the refrigerater overnight. Bake at 400 degrees for about 30 minutes – until golden brown.

Cool a bit after baking and slice on the diagonal into pieces that are about ¾" wide.

Note:

The salmon pastry can be served warm or at room temperature. Have a small bowl of sour cream alongside for guests who may like a spoonful on top.

Easy Shrimp Scampi

This recipe can be used as an appetizer or entrée when served over cooked rice or tossed with fettucini or spaghetti.

You Will Need:

1½ pounds medium shrimp (about 24 depending on size)

⅓ cup butter

¼ cup minced garlic

6 green onions, sliced

¼ cup dry white wine

2 tablespoons fresh lemon juice

2 tablespoons fresh parsley, minced

Salt and pepper to taste

Shell and devein shrimp, rinse briefly, drain on paper towels and set aside. Heat butter over medium heat. Cook garlic a few minutes until softened but not brown. Add shrimp, onions, wine and lemon juice and cook until shrimp are pink and firm, about 2 minutes. Do not overcook as it will cause the shrimp to be tough. Remove from heat and add parsley and salt and pepper. I serve four of the shrimp on tiny oval dishes with some of the sauce drizzled over the top.

This will serve 6 as an appetizer or four as an entrée over rice or pasta.

Pasta with Crab Sauce

You Will Need:

Dungeness or other meaty crabs

1 cup chopped onion

3 cloves garlic, smashed

Olive oil to coat bottom of pot

1 28 ounce can crushed tomatoes

1 28 ounce can tomato sauce

¼ cup tomato paste

1 tablespoon oregano

2 tablespoon parsley

1 pound linguini or spaghetti

The size and availability of Dungeness crabs varies so widely that it is impossible to give exact amounts of how much you should buy. Sometimes even the weight does not determine the amount of meat that a crab will yield. I will say that if the crabs are small, two would serve two people and if they are large, two would serve three or four. You could buy crabmeat to supplement although it is very expensive when bought that way.

It is a good idea to start early getting the crab ready for the pot. You and your helper can pull off all of the legs and separate the joints. Save the tiny joint at the end for stock and scrape the hairs off the others with a sharp paring knife. Scrub them, cut a small slit in each one and set aside. Crack the body of the crab and pick out all of the meat. Refrigerate this in a separate bowl. If you are lucky enough to have a good fish market, they will usually remove the plate that runs across the bottom and dispose of the gray jelly that is inside.

To make the sauce, heat the olive oil in a large pot over medium heat and sauté the onion and garlic until soft and golden. Add the crab legs and let them cook for about 4-5 minutes, stirring them occasionally. Add the tomato products and ½ cup of water. Season with oregano, parsley, salt and pepper to taste and continue cooking at a low simmer for about 45 minutes. You can keep the sauce warm while you are cooking the pasta.

Note:

Have enough nutcrackers and picks at the table so that each person can crack the legs. They are very tasty, especially if you lose your inhibitions and suck the meat out of each one.

In a large pot cook the pasta following directions on the package. When it is al dente drain and put it back into the pot with enough of the sauce to coat it.

Serve in large shallow bowls with some extra sauce. Arrange some of the leg pieces around the edges and some of the crab meat on top in the center.

Fruit Stuffed Pork Loin

This roast requires the large pork loin that is around 4" in diameter. Although this cut is not quite as tender as the pork tenderloin it is still excellent and stuffing it makes for an impressive presentation. Most of the work can be done the day before or you can freeze it after the prep and thaw and roast when you need it.

Pork should be cooked only to the slightly pink stage. Cooking it longer will make it tough and dry. An instant read meat thermometer will allow you to determine when it reaches 160 degrees, the point at which any possible bacterial problems would be eliminated.

You Will Need:

A 3-4 pound boneless pork loin

16-18 dried prunes

16-18 dried apricots

4-5 garlic cloves

Salt and pepper to taste

1 stick softened butter

3 tablespoons thyme

1½ cups red wine

¼ cup molasses

If you are using a whole pork loin that has not been cut and tied you will need to use a very long sharp knife to make an opening running through the center of the loin lengthwise. You may have to do this from each end to get to the center. Then, with the handle of a long wooden spoon push dried apricots and prunes, alternately, into the opening. You may need to do this from both ends also.

Cut four or five garlic cloves into slivers and poke these into deep cuts that you have made in the top of the roast. With some paper towels, dry the top of the roast well and season it with salt and freshly ground pepper. Smear it generously with softened butter and pat dried thyme into the butter coating. Refrigerate (or freeze) until ready to use.

Note:

Being aware of the origin of the cuts of meat you are buying will help you choose what will work best for your recipe. My butchers are more than accommodating and recently, when I asked one for a quick lesson on a pork tenderloin I was buying, he brought out a whole slab of the loin still attached to the backbone. He showed me that it sits under a layer of fat and is pretty tender because it really does not have to work hard and does not develop muscle. Attached to it is a small loin which is the most tender piece of all and is aptly named tenderloin. The big loin is around 4" in diameter and the small one is less than half that size. Being in shorter supply, it is naturally more expensive.

Pork is often advertised as "the other white meat" because the chops and some of the roasts are very lean. However, if you like the juiciness of the darker cuts, and can tolerate the fat that surrounds something like a shoulder roast, you will experience a more intense flavor and a very tender texture. This lends itself well to shredding for pulled pork.

To roast, place the meat in a shallow roasting pan. Mix together the red wine and molasses and pour it over the roast. Bake at 350 for about 1½ hours, basting occasionally. Remove from oven and allow it to rest, loosely covered with aluminum foil. Then cut thick slices and place them back in pan with the sauce that is remaining in the pan. Return the meat, covered, to a 250 oven while you are finishing off the other food you are serving, about 20 minutes. You may have to add a bit more liquid if the pan is dry. You could use wine or chicken broth or just a bit of water. This will moisten the meat. Overlap the slices on a platter with the sauce poured over them.

Easiest Pork Tenderloin

This is a very simple recipe and it is worth it to fix the whole thing because the leftovers make great sandwiches. Each tenderloin usually weighs between 1 and 1½ pounds or a bit more. They often are sold in a vacuum sealed package holding two tenderloins. Ask your butcher to split a package of them if you want to buy only one.

You Will Need:

2 Pork Tenderloins

4 tablespoons softened butter

2-3 tablespoons dried or fresh thyme

Olive oil to coat sauté pan

2-3 large smashed garlic cloves, peeled

½ cup or more red wine

Salt and pepper to taste

Pat the tenderloins dry with paper towels and then salt and pepper them. Rub each one all over with 2 tablespoons softened butter. Generously coat them with thyme. You can do this preparation early in the day and cover and refrigerate them. When ready to cook, heat enough olive oil on medium high to coat the bottom of a sauté pan. Make sure you are using a pan that can be transferred to the oven (no plastic handle). Sear the meat, turning so that it is browned all over. Toward the end of searing, add the smashed garlic cloves to the skillet. When the meat is nicely browned, remove it to a plate and add the wine to the skillet. Bring to a boil and loosen any tidbits from the bottom of the pan.

Remove from heat and return tenderloin to the pan. Place in a 350 oven for about 20-30 minutes. Remove from the oven and loosely cover with foil for about 15 minutes. Slice to serve and pour any remaining sauce over top.

Note:

Searing is an extremely important part of meat preparation. It holds the juices in and must be done over heat that is high enough to quickly lend a deep brown crust to each side of the meat. On my stove the temperature is set on an eight out of ten. If you do a slower browning the juices will seep out of the meat and you will almost be poaching it. The end result will be dry and gray looking. If the finished tenderloin is too pink for your taste, you can pop it in a 375 oven for a few minutes after it is sliced.

Sometimes searing can result in grease splatters on you and your stovetop. A wire mesh splatter lid can help to eliminate this problem while still allowing the steam to escape.

Pork Shoulder Roast

Once this roast is prepared for the oven, it will cook with very little attention. The fat allows the roast to do most of its own basting and the end product is very juicy and flavorful. If you are concerned about the fat content, much of it can be cut away for serving. I don't cook this often but it is so delicious I just consider it an occasional sinful indulgence.

You Will Need:

3-4 pound pork shoulder roast, bone in or boneless

3-4 large garlic cloves

2 tablespoons thyme, fresh or dried

Coarse sea salt and freshly ground pepper

Dry roast off with paper towels and cut deep slits all along the top of the roast. Peel garlic and cut lengthwise into slivers. Sprinkle salt and pepper on all sides of roast and then turn it so that you can push garlic slivers into each slit. Rub the thyme into the top of roast.

Place in a roasting pan and cook in a 350 oven, uncovered, for about 3½ hours. Check it at about 3 hours to see if it is done. You can cut off a tiny piece to taste. The roast should be moist and tender. With a very sharp knife cut it into thick slices, lay them back in pan and cover loosely with foil. You do not want the meat to steam, only to stay warm while you are preparing last minute things for the meal.

Note:

While the pork is roasting, you could scrub some russet potatoes, cut a few slits in them and let them bake on the racks of the oven. You'll have an easy dinner with a salad and maybe a green vegetable or some sautéed apple slices.

Baby Back Ribs

This is a recipe that I got many years ago from Elaine, a family friend who golfed in my mother's foursome. If they needed a fourth when I was home from college I occasionally filled in. I fit right in with their skill level and I particularly liked their suggestions such as "Oh, that wasn't you – take that one over" or "Let's just give you a five". I found out later that we had to turn in our scorecards at the luncheon so that they could determine who won.

I golfed so infrequently that I held to the hope that no one in the club would connect me with the ladies with the impossibly low scores. If nothing else we did laugh a lot and Elaine was the funniest one there. I liked that she always said I looked like I belonged in her family. She was Jewish and a wonderful cook (in her obviously non Kosher kitchen) and I think of her every time I make these ribs.

You Will Need:

Two racks of baby back pork ribs

1 large onion, quartered and chopped

Salt and pepper

½ cup brown sugar

¼ cup Worcestershire sauce

2 cups water

¼ cup white or cider vinegar

1 cup ketchup (I'm a Heinz fan, maybe because I got a pickle pin at the factory when I was a kid.)

To prepare, cut the ribs into individual pieces and spread them out in a large shallow pan or two smaller ones. Sprinkle well with salt and pepper. Scatter onions over the top of the ribs. Cook uncovered for 30-40 minutes in a 400 oven until lightly brown.

While they are browning, combine the brown sugar, Worcestershire sauce, water, vinegar and ketchup. Bring mixture to a boil over medium high heat, lower heat and simmer for 15 minutes.

Remove the ribs from the oven and pour off any accumulated fat. Pour

Note:

For preparing ribs you will have consistently good results with the baby back ribs. Because of their smaller size they are easier to cut into serving pieces and are more tender than the ribs from a larger animal. Again they are more expensive but worth it.

¾ of the sauce over top of the ribs and bake uncovered in a 350 oven for 1½ hours, basting occasionally and turning them a few times. The sauce should thicken and the ribs will turn a deep brown. If you need the rest of the sauce, add it while they are cooking. If not, save it for reheating the ribs if you are doing them the day before.

To reheat the ribs, pour a bit of the reserved sauce over top, cover with foil and place in a 350 oven until heated through.

Marinated Roast Lamb

Lamb is best on the rare side so be sure to check after an hour and 15 minutes so that it is not overdone. Read through the recipe before you go to the meat market and decide if you want to prepare it tied or laid out flat.

You Will Need:

1 leg of Lamb, 4-5 pounds after boning

2 tablespoon peppercorns (black or mixture of black, green and white)

2 tablespoons fresh or dried rosemary

6 coarsely chopped garlic cloves

½ cup raspberry vinegar

¼ cup soy sauce

½ cup red wine

Dijon mustard

For the marinade: Combine coarsely ground peppercorns, rosemary, garlic cloves, raspberry vinegar, soy sauce, and red wine.

Marinate lamb for at least 8 hours, untied, turning occasionally, in a non-reactive dish or in a plastic zip bag.

Remove lamb from marinade and roll and tie it. Pat it dry enough to thinly coat it with Dijon mustard and more coarsely ground pepper to taste. Set in a shallow roasting pan and pour marinade around but not over roast. Bake at 350, uncovered, for 1½ hours (18 minutes a pound).

If you prefer to cook it on your outdoor grill leave it untied and grill it according to instructions for your particular grill. I prefer to brush it with the reserved marinade and sear it quickly on high on both sides and then use an indirect medium heat for the remaining time. A 4 pound cut will take about 50-60 minutes.

Remove to a platter and loosely cover with foil for 20 minutes before carving. The roast may absorb some of the pan juices as it sits. Pour whatever liquid or marinade (if grilling) is left into a skillet. Bring to a slow boil and whisk in a few tablespoons of butter a few bits at a time until it is well blended. Serve in a gravy boat with the lamb.

Note:

This is a good time to make use of your meat thermometer. Keep the roast under 140 degrees so that it is deliciously juicy. You can always cook it further but there is no going back when you cook it too long.

Boudin Blanc

I serve sliced Boudin Blanc as part of a breakfast buffet. It's a very lightly seasoned white sausage that is made with chicken and cream and bread-crumbs and sometimes a bit of veal or pork. It is heavenly. I first tasted this at a café in Eugene where they offered the sausages as a part of the brunch menu. You won't find them at most grocery stores but you might try a good meat market where they possibly make their own. It's worth the hunt.

Place sausages in a skillet coated with olive oil and turn until lightly browned. Then let them cook further in a 350 oven for 20–25 minutes. Cut into chunks for serving.

SOUTHERN FRIED CHICKEN AND FRENCH FRIED POTATOES

Back in the 50's families we knew didn't go on real vacations. Most, like us, went to visit their relatives, whether it was only a day trip or sometimes longer. Occasionally in the summer we would go to New Jersey to visit my mother's brother who also had a place at Greenwood Lake, New York.

Our trips were always by car and much of it was by way of the Pennsylvania Turnpike. The highway system was in its infancy and it was monotonous, not much to look at, especially after dark. The three of us girls slept for a while with two on the back seat and one on the floor, which had a hump in the center that made it impossible to get comfortable. My mother always packed sandwiches and fruit but our treat was stopping at Howard Johnson's, the first turnpike restaurant in the United States. This was our chance to use the bathroom since my Dad was notorious for speeding up when he thought we might spot a rest stop.

I don't remember the food at Howard Johnson's or if we even ate there. My memory is of the 28 flavors of ice cream that we could choose from before we left the place. That was way too much pressure – I couldn't decide and I probably ended up with something safe like chocolate.

Our longer car trip was when we actually went all the way to Florida. What a thing to do! At my grade school my least favorite subject was geography and I hadn't seen any maps or heard any explanations other than it would take us about three days to get there. And we would stay in an apartment that had two bedrooms, a small kitchen and bathroom and it was right on the beach.

The only information that I remember my Dad passing on to us involved food. When we passed through Virginia he talked about ham and said that we would pick one up on the way home. The Carolinas weren't very interesting but Georgia was the best place to buy some peaches and we would stop for dinner there too. That was when I had my very first taste of Southern Fried Chicken and French Fried Potatoes. It was a magnificent experience – maybe the best thing I had ever tasted, and it was so good that I ordered it every single time we went out for dinner. No bothering with a menu, I knew what I wanted. I ate so much chicken that, when my Dad would tell friends about our trip, he would always say that Pauline Jean ate seven chickens. A slight exaggeration but who was counting!

I don't even try to duplicate the Southern Fried Chicken that I had that summer. For me, it would be like copying the Mona Lisa. It was that good. So here are a few recipes that are easier and very tasty.

Chicken on a Busy Day

This recipe easily serves four people. It is the quickest way I know of to prepare a chicken dinner. I like thighs but if you are using the breasts cut them in half crosswise. The cooking time may vary a bit depending on the size of the chicken pieces so try to keep them uniform.

You Will Need:

8 pieces of chicken

2 tablespoons butter

2 tablespoons olive oil

Rosemary or thyme or an herb of your choice

Salt and pepper to taste

Trim any excess fat from the chicken pieces, saving the trimmings in a freezer bag for your next batch of broth. Rinse the chicken and pat it dry. In a large skillet, heat the butter and oil on medium high. Without crowding, place the chicken pieces skin side down, turning when each piece is golden brown. Do not crowd the chicken – it is better to brown it in two batches. When both sides are golden place the pieces skin side down in a shallow baking dish. Scatter the herb and salt and pepper over top.

Place the chicken in a 375 oven and bake for about 30 minutes. Turn the chicken once more so that it is skin side up. Bake for another 15 minutes. If the skin isn't as crispy as you would like turn on the broiler for about 5 minutes and place the baking pan a few inches from the heat elements.

Chicken Pot Pie

This is the best pot pie I have ever had. It is a real comfort food and is a dish I make when I am preparing chicken stock for soup. Use the chicken soup recipe in this book or use a high quality commercial broth (low salt if you can get it).

You Will Need:

2 cups chicken broth

7 tablespoons butter

7 tablespoons flour

1 teaspoon Worcestershire

1 cup half and half or whole milk

2 tablespoons finely chopped parsley

1 teaspoon tarragon

Salt and pepper to taste

1½ cups cooked sliced carrots from the soup or cooked separately if using a commercial broth

2 cups blanched frozen peas

3 cups of chicken from the soup or otherwise cooked, in ½" chunks

To assemble the pot pie, you will first make a white sauce. Melt the butter in a saucepan and then whisk in the flour. Add half and half or whole milk, chicken broth and Worcestershire. Whisk over medium heat until thickened. Remove from heat and stir in finely chopped parsley, tarragon and salt and pepper to taste.

Add chicken, carrots and peas to the sauce. Spoon into a 10 cup oval casserole dish or one of comparable capacity. Top with Southern Buttermilk Biscuits (recipe in this book). Bake uncovered at 425 degrees for 25-30 minutes. The sauce should be bubbly and the biscuits golden.

Breaded Chicken

I am always happy to find something that has the grandkids asking for seconds. This is one of those dishes.

You Will Need:

2-3 pounds boneless skinless chicken breasts or thighs

1 cup seasoned bread crumbs

½ cup plain bread crumbs

¼ cup finely grated Parmesan or Romano

2 tablespoons finely minced parsley

1-2 eggs, beaten with 1 tablespoon water

Canola oil and olive oil in equal amounts to coat skillet

Cut each breast in half crosswise and then, between two sheets of plastic wrap, pound them to about ¼" thick. If you are using thighs they may not need much pounding. Cut the meat into the size pieces that you like, maybe smaller for the kids.

On a plate combine the bread crumbs, grated cheese and parsley. In a shallow bowl beat an egg or two with a tablespoon of cold water. Swish the chicken pieces in the egg mix and then press both sides of each piece into the bread crumb mixture. Place the breaded chicken on a tray and refrigerate, covered, for 20 minutes or more to let the crumbs set.

Coat the bottom of a large skillet to about ¼ inch with the oil mixture. Heat on medium high and first test the temperature by setting a small piece of breaded chicken in it. It should start browning without absorbing oil. If it is ready, lay the prepared pieces in without crowding the skillet. They should turn golden brown in a few minutes. Turn and let the other side brown lightly. Remove to a paper towel lined baking sheet to remove any excess oil. When finished with the cooking, place the breasts in a shallow baking pan that will hold them in one layer.

Bake at 375 for about 15–20 minutes. Sprinkle with salt and pepper to taste and serve.

Note:

My pounder is designed very simply. It is a round disc 2¾" in diameter that weighs about 1¼ pounds. The handle is in the center and allows you to evenly flatten the filet just using a straight up and down motion.

Mediterranean Chicken & Pasta

This is a great big recipe that is perfect for a potluck or party. It makes 10-12 generous servings and is good at room temperature. If there are any leftovers, they will keep well in the refrigerator. Or, if you prefer, the recipe is an easy one to cut in half.

You Will Need:

1 pound penne pasta, cooked and drained

1½ pounds roasted boneless chicken breasts, cubed or cut into strips

8 ounces Feta cheese, crumbled

1½ cups pitted Kalamata olives

1 teaspoon dried oregano

¾ cup diced oil packed sundried tomatoes

½ cup diced roasted red peppers

6 ounce bag of baby spinach leaves, uncooked, with stems removed

1 cup asiago salad dressing (I use Annie's)

½ cup coarsely grated Parmesan or Romano cheese

In a very large bowl combine all ingredients except the dressing and the coarsely grated cheese. Then add half of the dressing and toss well. Add enough of the other half to your own taste.

Spoon into several attractive serving dishes and scatter the Parmesan or Romano over the top.

Note:

If you don't have a commercial sized stainless steel mixing bowl, you can pick one up for a few dollars at your local thrift store. You will find that it is perfect not only for this recipe but for the rice salad, pizza and cinnamon rolls that are also in this book.

French Bread Farci

NOTE:

If you are freezing these, thaw for an hour before baking, adding 5 or 10 minutes to the baking time.

These little sandwiches are very good and they are perfect for a game party or a picnic. You can make them early in the day and refrigerate them or freeze them for even later use.

You Will Need:

One package of 12 French rolls (about 4" long)

½ cup water

¼ cup minced fresh parsley

3 tablespoons Dijon mustard

2 eggs, lightly beaten

½ teaspoon dried oregano

Freshly ground pepper to taste

One pound mild pork sausage

One pound ground chuck

1 medium onion, diced

6 tablespoons melted butter

2 cloves garlic, minced

Halve rolls lengthwise. Using your fingers, remove soft centers, leaving shells about ¼" thick. Break up the bread and lay it out on a baking sheet to dry or set it in a 250 oven for 20-30 minutes. Transfer it to a bowl and add water, parsley, mustard, eggs, oregano and pepper. Mix well and set aside.

Brown sausage, beef, and onion in a large skillet over medium high heat; breaking up the meat as it cooks. When meat is cooked through and onion is soft, drain well. Combine meat and crumb mixture and blend thoroughly. Divide equally among rolls, packing slightly and place on an ungreased baking sheet. Melt butter with garlic and brush over filling and edges of bread.

Bake in a 400 oven for 10 or 15 minutes or until hot and golden brown.

Ham, Cheese, & Spinach Bread Pudding

You Will Need:

One large baguette, day old

¼ cup melted butter

1 large onion, sliced thinly

1 pound cooked ham, roughly cut

2 tablespoons olive oil

4 large eggs

2 cups half and half

2 cups whole milk

½ teaspoon salt

¼ teaspoon nutmeg, optional

¼ pound cheese, shredded (Fontina is mild and smooth and melts beautifully but choose what you like)

6 cups spinach leaves, coarsely chopped

Note:

This can actually be assembled ahead of time, even the night before if you are using it for breakfast.

Diagonally slice bread ¾ inch thick and brush both sides with butter. Toast on a cookie sheet under broiler about 3" from heat. Turn once to lightly brown both sides.

Saute onion in oil over medium heat, stirring occasionally until golden brown. When almost done, add ham and stir until ham is mixed well.

Whisk eggs in a large bowl and add the milk and half and half, salt and nutmeg. Add a few toasted bread slices at a time to liquid and remove quickly to a shallow 3 quart casserole, overlapping them in rows. Use a spatula to lift slices a bit and tuck the ham, spinach and a bit of the cheese between the slices.

Pour remaining egg mixture evenly over the casserole and sprinkle with more of the shredded cheese.

Bake in a 350 oven for 45-55 minutes until puffed and golden.

Mac & Cheese

This recipe makes enough for 12 servings. You could divide the recipe in half, but since you are taking the time to go through all the steps, you may as well make it all and freeze some. The whole recipe fills a three quart casserole but I divide it into 4 smaller baking dishes and freeze those unbaked. Use whatever sizes suit your purposes that will add up to 3 quarts. When ready to use one, thaw almost completely and bake until bubbly and golden on top.

You Will Need:

6 thick slices of coarse day old bread, crusts removed

3 tablespoons melted butter

5½ cups whole milk

6 tablespoons butter

½ cup flour

1½ teaspoons salt

¼ teaspoon nutmeg (optional)

Coarsely ground pepper to taste

4½ cups sharp white cheddar, coarsely grated

1¼ cups finely grated Romano or Parmesan

1 pound elbow macaroni or small bowties, if you like

Pull small chunks, around ¼", from bread slices and place them in a medium bowl. Pour 2 tablespoons melted butter over bread, toss and set aside.

Butter the baking dish(es) of your choice.

Warm milk over medium heat but do not boil. While milk is warming melt 6 tablespoon butter in high sided skillet. Add the flour and whisk in for a minute.

Slowly pour warm milk into the mixture, a cup or so at a time, whisking to keep it smooth. When the milk is incorporated, continue whisking and cooking for about 10 minutes until bubbling and thickened. It will be the thickness of buttermilk. Remove from heat and add 3 cups of the cheddar and 1 cup of Romano/Parmesan. Set the sauce aside.

Cook your pasta to barely al dente (it will cook a bit more in the oven), drain it and add it to the sauce.

Transfer to your buttered baking dishes.

Mix together the remaining 1½ cups cheddar and ¼ cup Parmesan or Romano. Sprinkle over the top of the casserole and then scatter the prepared bread crumbs over this.

Bake at 375 for 30 minutes or until bubbly and golden brown on top. Transfer to a rack for 5 minutes and serve.

Pastas & Pizzas

SOUTHERN ITALIAN COOKING

When I have the time I teach cooking classes because I like to show people how simple it is to prepare an authentic Italian dinner for their families. I jumped right into it many years ago with my first venture being a six week class at River Road Park. Four of my students were my friends and the other four were new to me. The class started with appetizers and moved on to pasta and sauce, entrees, soups, vegetables and desserts. The students worked in pairs at the four stoves and the rule was that they changed partners every week to ensure that one person would not dominate the cooking process.

I got great reviews but in my overzealousness I brought more and more ingredients for the students to try. I ended up making $30.00 for my six weeks of work but it was enough to buy a very large spaghetti pot at the restaurant supply store. Thirty years later I still have that pot – it is magnificent and indestructible and a reminder of a very sweet time.

My subsequent classes have been occasional and are held in my home. I can only accommodate six students and we have a lesson and dinner. Mostly they are young women who have jobs and a family so I try to stress the fun part of cooking and the fact that making a mistake is not the end of the world. I am happy when they tell me later that they have successfully prepared the dishes for their family and some have even taught their husbands the techniques.

Pasta Sauce

The traditional pasta sauce of the Abruzzi region of Italy is the one my family always served and, when I went to Italy, I found that in Abruzzi it tasted exactly the same as what I had always eaten. I would suggest that you make this sauce in abundance. It freezes beautifully and will also keep in the refrigerator for a week or more.

You Will Need:

Olive oil, about ¼ cup to coat bottom of the pot

2 pounds thick pork shoulder chops, cut into 4-5 pieces

Beef neck bone, optional

1 onion chopped

5-6 garlic cloves, smashed

32 ounces tomato sauce

32 ounces crushed tomatoes

3-4 tablespoons tomato paste

1½ cups water

2-3 tablespoons sugar

Salt and pepper to taste

2 tablespoons dried basil

1 tablespoon dried oregano

¼ cup finely chopped fresh parsley or 2 tablespoons dried

The essential ingredient is pork and the best cut would be pieces of the shoulder with some bone attached. You will often find boneless country ribs, which actually come from the shoulder, in the market. If you have an accommodating butcher, ask to have some pieces cut with the bone in. This will give added flavor to your sauce.

Coat the bottom of a large pot with olive oil and heat to medium high. Dry off the pork with a paper towel and sear the pieces in the oil, turning as each side browns. You can season them with salt and pepper as you are searing. Remove the meat when it is browned and set it aside. Turn

Note:

In this country, pasta is often served swimming in sauce. You will have a much better experience if, after draining your pasta, you put it back in the pot and mix enough of the sauce with it to coat it a bit. Then, just ladle enough sauce on top of each serving without drowning it. You do want to taste the pasta too. Serve with some reggiano grated on top. Have extra sauce and extra cheese at the table for those who feel they need it.

I would suggest that you buy the intensely flavorful tomato paste that is sold in 4½ ounce tubes. It is more expensive but you will have no waste since it will last for a very long time in the refrigerator. I use an Italian product called Amore that is very good. The tomato sauces that are from Italy are typically of very good quality. The Pomi brand is excellent and there are some other products that indicate that they are from San Marzano which is the premier tomato growing area of Italy. You can also get good tomato products from this country, particularly the Hunt's brand which has expanded to include organic.

Standing in front of my grand-mother's childhood home in Roseto Valfortore.

the heat to medium and add the onion and garlic which will give off a bit of moisture that helps to loosen the bits of meat that may be clinging to the bottom of the pot. Cook until soft and lightly golden, stirring occasionally. At this point add the crushed tomatoes and the tomato sauce. Squeeze the tomato paste into one of the empty cans, add ½ cup of water and whisk this around to get all of the product out. Use another cup of water to clean out the cans, adding this water to the sauce. Season with basil and oregano and fresh parsley (or 2 tablespoons of dried). Also add sugar to the pot and salt and pepper to taste.

Return seared meat to sauce and bring it to a simmer. Let this slowly cook with the lid partially on for about an hour and a half, stirring occasionally to keep it from sticking. Then turn off the heat and let the pot sit on the back of the stove, covered, for a few hours or more. Don't worry about doing this. The acid in the tomatoes will marinate the meat and help to tenderize it and when you continue the cooking, bringing the heat to a simmer will return the sauce to a safe temperature.

An hour or so before serving, reheat the sauce on medium low with the browned meatballs if you choose to make them. Simmer and stir occasionally during this time so that the sauce does not burn on the bottom.

Serve the pork, cut into small chunks, on a platter at the table or, if you are preparing individual plates, place some on top of each serving of pasta. Add a meatball or serve those in a bowl at the table.

Meatballs

This is a recipe that you can double or triple or change to suit your taste. You may want to make a lot of these meatballs because they freeze well. A pound and a half of meat will make about 16 meatballs.

You Will Need:

1½ pounds ground beef or 1 pound beef and ½ pound pork

2 large eggs

2 tablespoons minced parsley or 1 tablespoon dried

3 tablespoons finely grated Parmesan or Romano

1½-2 cups stale coarse bread, moistened

Salt and pepper

Olive oil for coating skillet

For the 1½ pounds of meat, you will first need some stale bread. A good rustic loaf is best. Trim off the crusts a bit because they don't break down well. Place some chunks of bread in a bowl with enough water to cover. Let it sit a minute to absorb some water and then squeeze out as much of it as possible. You should have about 1½-2 cups of crumbly bread. In a large bowl combine bread, eggs, grated Romano or Parmesan, parsley and salt and pepper to taste. Work this bread mixture well and, if you aren't averse to using your hands, you will get a good feel of when the mixture is homogeneous. It will be kind of like oatmeal.

Next step, add the meat and take your time working the ingredients until they are completely blended. Form the meatballs so that they are about the size of a medium plum.

To cook, coat a skillet with a little olive oil and heat to medium high. Place some of the meatballs in the pan—do not crowd—and turn them as they brown. Watch closely and use a small spatula to gently turn them. They may look like they have flattened a bit but they will round out when cooked in the sauce.

Remove onto paper towels and continue browning the rest.

To freeze, place them on a baking sheet that is lined with waxed paper. Freeze until firm and store in zip bags. To use, thaw first and then put them in the simmering sauce. They will need to cook for about an hour.

Note:

I use the 15% fat content ground beef and I like to buy a good local grass fed brand. It costs a bit more but there is a noticeable difference in flavor.

Marinara

I make a meatless sauce to use with manicotti, gnocchi, pasta or eggplant parmigiana, especially if I am having guests who are vegetarians. It is easy and is a good alternative to the meat entrees.

You Will Need:

Olive Oil to coat bottom of a deep saucepan (about ¼ cup)

One large onion, chopped

3 or four cloves garlic, smashed

32 ounce can of crushed tomatoes

32 ounce can of tomato sauce

A few tablespoons of tomato puree

1 cup or so of water

2 tablespoons dried basil or ¼ cup minced fresh

1 tablespoon oregano

¼ cup fresh parsley, minced

2 tablespoons sugar

Salt and pepper to taste

Coat a deep saucepan or pot with olive oil and add the onion and garlic. Let these cook until soft and lightly golden. Add the tomatoes and water. Stir well and add the herbs and sugar.

Let this simmer for about 45 minutes. You will not need as much water as the meat sauce since the cooking time is shorter and the water will not be dissipating as much. You can make this early in the day and leave it at room temperature. There is nothing in it that could have a bad reaction.

Gnocchi

I once said, in a moment of deep reflection of course, that if I could have one item with me on a deserted island, I would choose gnocchi. I thought this was a reasonable answer to a simple question until one of my daughters pointed out that a solar blanket or Swiss army knife might be more useful.

Needless to say, a plate of gnocchi is my very favorite dinner in the world and I am sticking to my guns on that desert island thing. So, although the recipe may sound complicated, I hope you will try it. Each time you do, you will get better – guaranteed.

EVERYONE CAN MAKE GNOCCHI!

Procedure:

The following items are very helpful for making gnocchi:

A good sturdy ricer.

A very large work board or other clean, flat place.

Several cookie sheets covered with waxed paper or some plastic cutting mats.

A board scraper for cutting and transferring the gnocchi to the cookie sheets.

A fork for yourself and each person helping.

A large slotted scooper with a long handle.

Russet potatoes are best to use because they are dry and somewhat mealy and will be easy to press through the ricer. Try to find potatoes of similar size so they will finish cooking at approximately the same time. For every pound of potatoes you will need about 1 cup of flour. This includes the flour you will use during the rolling and cutting. For every 2-3 pounds of potatoes you will use one large egg. We will proceed with 3 pounds.

First scrub the potatoes and boil them whole with the skins on. They will absorb less water than if you peeled them. When each potato is tender but not mushy, remove from water. Push a sharp knife into the center of each one to check for doneness. Leave them to cool enough so that you can peel the skins off.

Note:

The leftover gnocchi is still very good when reheated the next day. Just add a small bit of water and cover and place in a 300 oven until heated through.

When the potatoes are at room temperature press them through the ricer onto a floured work surface forming a mound as you work. Make a well in the center. Sprinkle a few teaspoons of salt and a cup of flour over top and drop one egg into the center. Work these ingredients together so that the flour is incorporated and then continue kneading in more flour until it takes on the feel of bread dough. You will want it to be firm enough to form ropes that don't flatten when you are rolling them.

When the dough is firm shape it into a big ball and coat it with some flour. You will also be coating the gnocchi with a bit of flour as you are rolling and forming them. Cut off a chunk of dough that is about 1½ cups and gently roll it into a rope to about a ¾" diameter, being careful to not push down when you are rolling. Cut and roll several more chunks and line them up against each other. Cut into pieces not quite ¾" long. Then, and here's the tricky part, hold a fork with the tines on the board at a 45 degree angle. Roll the pieces of dough down the fork using the tips of your index and middle finger – gently pushing down just enough to propel it down the fork. This will give the gnocchi a shell shape which allows them to cook more evenly. And they look prettier.

Always keep flour handy to sprinkle over the gnocchi so they don't become sticky. Sprinkle some of the flour on your cookie sheets and then transfer gnocchi on to these as they are formed. Try to keep them separated from each other.

To cook, bring salted water to a boil in a very large pot. When the water is at a rolling boil, carefully slide the gnocchi into the water, cooking one tray of them at a time. With a long wooden spoon very gently stir them a little—they will have sunk to the bottom so you don't want them to stick together. Adjust the water to a slow boil and watch as the gnocchi rise to the top. Let them boil gently for a minute or two and using your long handled slotted strainer remove them from the water. Before transferring them to a large serving dish that has been coated with some pasta sauce I rinse them under a slow stream of cold water. This is the only pasta that I rinse a bit when I pull them from the water. They are coated with flour and the water that they are cooking in becomes somewhat starchy. I like to remove any of that residue that remains on the gnocchi before I coat them with the sauce. Gently stir them around to distribute the sauce—a large rubber spatula is good for this—and transfer to a 200 oven to keep warm while the rest are cooking. Repeat this until all are cooked. Serve with some sauce on top and a scattering of grated Reggiano cheese.

Ricotta Spinach Gnocchi

Although I prefer the more traditional potato gnocchi, these are very good and much easier to make. You can serve this type of gnocchi as a side dish or as an entrée. It works well with marinara sauce, a cream sauce or a simple butter one which makes it a good vegetarian option.

You Will Need:

1 pound fresh, steamed spinach, finely chopped

1 pound ricotta, drained

1 egg

½ cup flour plus extra for flouring your hands

1 teaspoon salt

½ cup finely grated Parmesan or Romano cheese

After thawing or steaming, remove the moisture from the spinach by placing it in the center of a fine cotton towel, folding the ends over and twisting in opposite directions over a sink or bowl. The liquid will drip through the towel.

Place the ricotta in a large bowl and add egg, flour, salt and the spinach. Stir until well combined. Fold in Reggiano or Romano cheese.

Keep your hands floured and make balls about the size of a large cherry with the mixture. Set these on a cookie sheet that is lined with lightly floured waxed paper.

Bring a large pot of salted water to a boil and carefully drop gnocchi in, using no more than would cover the bottom of the pot. As they rise to the top of the pot, remove with a slotted scoop and place them in a casserole that is coated with some of the sauce you are using. Repeat until all are cooked.

When ready to serve, top each serving with more sauce as desired.

Manicotti

This is a special dish and one that can be prepared weeks ahead and frozen with no change in the quality. You can also assemble them early in the day of your dinner and refrigerate, covered.

Remember when buying fresh spinach that you will buy at least 1 pound to compensate for the waste when stemming and sorting through it.

You Will Need:

For the Crepes:

2 cups flour

½ teaspoon salt

6 eggs

2 cups 2% milk (or one cup milk and 1 cup water)

4 tablespoon melted butter

In large mixer bowl, combine the flour and salt. In another bowl, mix together eggs and milk. Add this gradually to flour, being careful to beat after each addition to avoid any lumps. Then add 4 tablespoons melted butter and blend well. Let this sit for about an hour so that it becomes more homogeneous. It will also thicken up a bit. Before using, stir it with a whisk to be sure that there are no tiny flecks of flour that are not incorporated.

To cook these, I would recommend a 7-8" pan. I am lucky to have a copper one that is lined with stainless steel and does not stick. I don't usually use coated cook wear but, if all else fails, this would be a good time for it. Brush the pan with a little melted butter and set it on medium heat. When hot, pour a little less than ⅓ cup of batter in pan and quickly swirl it around to fit the bottom of the pan. If it does not fill the pan easily add a bit more water to the batter to thin it down. Cook on one side only and remove when the top does not have any wet spots. Do not be concerned if your first ones are not perfect – it happens sometimes so just keep on with the rest. Lay crepes on waxed paper or plastic cutting mats. After they cool they can be stacked until ready to fill.

Note:

If you want to have people serve themselves at a buffet, bake them in a shallow casserole that is attractive enough to take to the table. Two manicotti per person is more than enough, especially if you are serving additional offerings of meat or vegetables.

For the Filling:

12 ounces fresh spinach, steamed and finely chopped

4 cups ricotta, drained of extra moisture

2 large eggs

¾ cup finely grated Romano or Parmesan

1½ cups grated mozzarella (use the large holes of a box grater)

Salt and pepper to taste

This filling can be prepared a day or two ahead. After the spinach is steamed you can remove any remaining moisture by laying it on the center of a cotton towel and folding the sides over it. Twist the ends of the towel in opposite directions to squeeze out the moisture. I keep an old smooth towel that I use only for tasks like this.

Stir eggs into the ricotta until well mixed. Add spinach, Parmesan or Romano, mozzarella and salt and pepper. If you mix this with your hands you can feel if the spinach is being evenly distributed. Cover and refrigerate.

When ready to assemble the manicotti, take a crepe and turn it so that the cooked side is up. Place a heaping tablespoon of the filling in the center and fold two sides in so that it looks like an open ended tube. Trim the ends and set manicotti on a plastic mat or a waxed paper lined baking sheet. Repeat until all crepes are used, laying manicotti side by side. Cover with plastic wrap and freeze if not using immediately. As soon as they are frozen, put them in freezer bags and store until ready to use.

To serve, lightly coat a baking dish with tomato sauce—the meat one in this book or a plain marinara. Arrange manicotti side by side and top with a light coating of sauce. Grate some Romano or Parmesan over top and bake for about 15-20 minutes at 350.

If you are using the frozen ones, thaw almost completely before baking. If they are refrigerated, let them sit at room temperature to take the chill off before baking.

Pesto Pasta

In summer and fall you can prepare lots of pesto from home grown basil. It is fast and easy to prepare and freezes beautifully. I like the flavor and the extra oiliness that comes from walnuts so often I substitute them for the pine nuts. I recently made this and added some small slices of leftover roasted chicken to the cooked pasta. It is a recipe that lends itself well to add-ons.

This dish looks and tastes great with a side dish of fresh tomatoes from the garden tossed with a bit of balsamic vinegar and minced fresh parsley.

You Will Need:

2 cups tightly packed basil leaves

1 cup pine nuts or walnuts

3 large cloves of garlic

¾ cup Reggiano or Romano, finely grated

⅔ cup extra virgin olive oil

Salt and pepper to taste

3 tablespoons heavy cream

2 tablespoons butter

2 tablespoons of hot water from the pasta

1 pound linguini or a pasta that will stand up to the thickness of the sauce

Wash and gently dry the basil. Drop it into a food processor along with the nuts and roughly cut garlic cloves. Chop until well combined. Continue blending while pouring the olive oil into the processor in a steady stream. Remove to a bowl and stir in the grated cheese. Add salt and pepper to taste, bearing in mind the saltiness of the cheese. Set this aside, covered, and cook the pasta. You can also fix the pesto a day or two ahead and refrigerate it with a plastic wrap laying directly on top of it. Keeping the air out will keep it from darkening too much

Boil the pasta so that it is al dente. When it is done scoop out 2 table-spoons of the hot water and add it to the pesto. Drain the pasta and return it to the pot with the butter. Toss the pasta so that it is coated a bit.

Mix two tablespoon of cream into the pesto and add it to the pasta. Toss until the pasta is well coated.

If you are cooking for two, half a pound of pasta and half of the pesto is more than enough. In that case freeze half of the pesto, leaving out the cheese in the portion that you are freezing. To ensure that the pesto does not discolor, store it in a container that is a tight fit. Place a piece of saran directly on the pesto and cover it and freeze. To use it, thaw, add the grated cheese and proceed.

ABOUT THE CHEESES

There is no hard and fast rule in choosing which grating cheese you are using. Just as the balsamic vinegar and olive oil productions are heavily monitored for quality in Italy, so too is the cheese production. In our markets we often see Parmigiana-Reggiano which is one of a category of cheese called Grana Padano. The Regianno is made from a rich and sweet unpasteurized cow's milk and it is aged longer and costs more than the other Granas which are still good, just not top of the line. The Pecorino family of cheeses encompasses the sharper and saltier offerings that are made with sheep's milk. If you want a bit of sharpness in your cooking Romano is a good choice for substituting or in combination with the Reggiano. Always check for saltiness before you add more salt to your recipe.

With the mozzarella you can use either the soft or hard variety. The soft one is milder and fresher tasting and melts beautifully in any recipe. It is a bit stickier on the grater.

Spaghetti Pie

This is a good way to use up leftovers and it is such an attractive dish that it is a good addition to any buffet table. Read through this recipe and you can assemble your own list of ingredients. You will have to coordinate the size of the skillet with the amount of spaghetti you are using. A 10" pan will hold about 5 cups of cooked pasta along with the vegetables. It's fun to put together and the end product will look nothing like last night's veggies.

Use your extra pasta from dinner or cook some up fresh. You will need, in addition to your other ingredients, enough to fill your skillet to a depth of about 1½ inches. You can use any pasta, but thin spaghetti or a small variety will give a more compact result.

In a large bowl, stir together the cooked pasta that is coated with a little spaghetti sauce, bits of leftover vegetables (like small pieces of cooked broccoli, peas and spinach), coarsely grated cheese such as mozzarella, cheddar or others with a mild flavor. Add ¼ cup of grated Parmesan and 3 beaten eggs. Mix this all together and then add a little more sauce.

Coat the bottom of a dependable skillet – one that doesn't stick and that cooks uniformly – with olive oil and heat to medium. Add spaghetti mixture to skillet and spread it out while keeping it packed together to make one whole pie.

Let this cook, watching the heat so that the bottom does not brown too much – a golden color is what you are after.

After this is done, slide the pie onto a large plate, place another plate on top and invert it. Then slide the pie back onto the skillet and cook until that side is golden and the ingredients are heated through and binding together.

To serve, slide onto a serving tray and let sit lightly covered for about 10 minutes before cutting into wedges. Spoon more tomato sauce over the top right before serving and sprinkle with more grated Parmesan.

Sicilian Style Pizza

The fabulous thing about this recipe is that the pizza dough can be pre-baked ahead of time, very handy if you are having a party and are busy with other last minute preparations.

You Will Need:

3 packages or 3 scant tablespoons yeast

1 cup warm water

2 cups water

1 cup milk

⅓ cup sugar

2 tablespoons salt

1 cup vegetable or canola oil

8-9 cups flour

Dissolve yeast in 1 cup warm water with a little sugar to proof it. Be sure that the yeast is good – you don't want to throw out this big mass of dough. Combine water, milk, sugar and salt in a saucepan and heat just until sugar dissolves. Pour this into a very large bowl and add 1 cup of vegetable oil. Add 4 cups flour and mix in well until fairly smooth. Add dissolved yeast, stir in and gradually add 4-5 more cups flour. Knead lightly until flour is incorporated—the kneading is more like just tossing it around until it looks homogeneous. It will not be as firm as bread dough. Let this rise until double—around one hour or a little more. With three tablespoons of yeast it will rise quickly.

Punch dough down and spread into oiled pans. You will have enough dough for two 11x15" pans and one round pizza pan.

When working with the dough, DO NOT pull it – you must be patient. Oil your hands and work alternately with all three pans. Push down gently with fingertips and work the dough to the edges of the pans. The dough will rest a little as you move from pan to pan. This may sound tedious but it is actually kind of therapeutic. You are relaxing while you are getting the dough to relax. Don't hurry!

You can refrigerate the pizzas with toppings or without as they will keep for a few days after the first baking. You can also wrap them tightly and freeze them for a few weeks or more. Let thaw for about an hour before baking.

A fun thing to do for a party is to have your guests assemble their own toppings which they can bring or you can have an assortment for them.

Top each pizza with a light coating of sauce and bake in a 375 oven for 15 or 20 minutes until very lightly brown. The pizzas should not feel doughy when touched but somewhat firm and raised. Remove from oven and when cool enough to handle, gently loosen pizza and remove from pan. Flip empty pan over and lay pizza on back side. You are now ready for the second baking. Baking the pizza on the back of the pan allows the edges to get more crispy.

Top with whatever you like – pepperoni, olives, mushrooms, onions – these are the first layer. Next, sprinkle a generous helping of medium grated mozzarella (fresh or hard), then spoon on a bit more sauce and spread gently (a fork works well for this). Lastly, top with finely grated Parmesan or Romano. Recently I have been topping one crust with a scattering of fresh spinach with sliced fresh mushrooms and tomatoes on top. The final touch is crumbled gorgonzola, however much you would like. It is delicious and more healthful than the more traditional variety. Bake again for about 15-20 minutes at 375 – checking it to make sure it is browned and not burned.

For the Sauce: If I have a few cups of my leftover spaghetti sauce, I will use that. Or, you can mix a good prepared pizza sauce with an equal amount of tomato sauce to tone it down a bit. You can also make a simple marinara with garlic, onion, basil, oregano, parsley and salt and pepper. It is, after all, just a pizza – so suit your own taste and have fun with it.

Fried Dough

This is something you can do with a portion of the Sicilian pizza dough (recipe in the entrée section of this book). If you make these once, your kids will want them every time you make pizza.

You Will Need:

Pizza dough, the one in this book

1½ inches of vegetable or canola oil

Sugar for sprinkling, mixed with a bit of cinnamon if you like

Save some of the dough from the pizza recipe, whatever meets your needs. In a deep skillet heat oil to medium high. Cut off pieces of dough, about the size of a golf ball. Stretch each piece out to around 4 inches and gently place it in the oil. You can usually do about four pieces at a time. Cook on both sides until golden, turning once. Remove from skillet, drain on paper towels and sprinkle with sugar while warm. My kids (and now grandkids) are usually standing around waiting for them so you may not even need a serving platter.

Note:

You can actually use the oil again since it won't be picking up any strong flavors or odors from the bread dough.

Breads & Breakfasts

MY DAD AND ME AND THE NEW TV

One day in the early 1950's my Dad had a really big surprise for us. It was a television set and it was such a new invention that I had never even thought of having one. Like everyone else we knew, we had a radio and we listened to The Lone Ranger, Henry Aldrich, The Shadow, Arthur Godfrey and my particular favorite, The Ted Mack Amateur Hour. I liked listening to the singers and comedians and even the tap dancers who could have been tapping with drumsticks for all I knew. I didn't know anyone who had a television and, when that magic moment came and my Dad turned it on, it was miraculous, like having a little movie screen in your own house.

It was so fascinating that I would watch practically anything – Kukla, Fran and Ollie and Howdy Doody or my Dad's westerns and boxing matches, baseball games and even the news reports.

In 1953 I witnessed a princess making her way slowly, with six young women holding a long, long cloak behind her, down the aisle of Westminster Abbey to be crowned as the new Queen of England.. The tape of the ceremony had been flown across the Atlantic so that it could be broadcast in the United States. As the crown was placed on Elizabeth's head, it was the most exciting thing this 12 year old girl had ever seen.

Not until 1961 did I see anything more stirring than that. It was when a vibrant young man named John Kennedy was sworn in as the 35th president of the United States. I was glued to the set, particularly since I had spent what should have been my study time campaigning for him. I saw him once, at a speaking event, so close I could touch his shoulder. And there he was, speaking to us, the new generation.

When we watched our programs together, my Dad was fair and he would read the paper while I turned on one of my shows, particularly American Bandstand. His only comment, with a smile on his face, was that "Those kids should be home helping their mothers fix dinner". At the time I was curled up in an easy chair while MY mother was in the kitchen fixing dinner.

The picture here was taken shortly after our TV arrived and I was chosen to pose like Betty Furness with her Westinghouse appliances. My Dad was the director, a friend was the photographer and I was the star. I wore my favorite dress and what appear to be my Dad's Florsheims. Someone told my mother that I needed orthopedic shoes because of my high arches and off we had gone to the Bostonian Shoe Store where I had my feet irradiated as I wiggled my toes and then I was fitted with these totally awful oxfords. I love the picture anyway.

Waffles

Almost forty years ago when we lived in what used to be the old farm area on the outskirts of Eugene there was an old house a few blocks from us on River Road. A huge sign in the front yard identified it as The Big Sail, a sort of permanent garage sale that was also the living quarters of a guy who was not a good speller. The place, inside and out, was stuffed with stuff. I was pulled to it in the way you might be drawn to an accident scene.

From the chaos inside I rescued a beautiful antique waffle iron that I was told was in great working condition. I was thinking "Is he kidding with the $20.00 price tag?" but I said "How about if I trade you a really nice sofa". I didn't tell him it didn't sell at my garage sale and I had no way of hauling it off. We struck a deal and my wonderful old appliance is still turning out waffles for family and friends. Hmm – I wonder how that sofa is doing.

I have seen many recipes for waffles that call for beaten egg whites that are folded into the batter. This one eliminates that step with no difference in the finished product. You will appreciate the simplicity of preparation and your family or guests will love the end result.

Note:

As you can see, it is easy math to cut this recipe in half. However, it may be worth it to fix the whole recipe and freeze the leftover waffles. Just pop them in the toaster to heat for a quick breakfast.

When I use a recipe that calls for buttermilk I feel very confident that it will turn out well. The end result is a tender product and one that works in concert with the leavening agent. If you bake frequently you may want to keep at least a pint of it on hand.

You Will Need:

4 eggs

2 cups buttermilk

2 cups flour

1 tablespoon baking powder

1 teaspoon baking soda

½ teaspoon salt

½ stick butter, melted

Additional melted butter for waffle iron

In a small bowl, whisk eggs with buttermilk. In a large bowl, combine dry ingredients and then add the egg mixture and melted butter. Whisk until blended. Follow the instructions for your waffle iron, using the amount of batter that it will hold. Brush some melted butter on the grids if your appliance calls for that.

Pancakes

You can eliminate or cut down on the sugar in this recipe (since you are probably going to serve the pancakes with syrup or berries) by incorporating a half cup of ripe mashed banana into the batter instead of the sugar.

You Will Need:

1 egg

1⅓ cup buttermilk

1½ cups flour

1 or 2 tablespoons sugar

1 teaspoon baking powder

¾ teaspoons soda

¼ cup butter, melted

Blueberries, optional

In a small bowl whisk the egg with the buttermilk. In another bowl combine flour, sugar, baking powder, salt and baking soda. Add the egg mixture to the flour along with the melted butter (or banana). If you melt the butter in the skillet in which you will cook the pancakes you can accomplish two things at once. Besides melting your ¼ cup of butter, your skillet will be oiled in the process.

Using low to medium heat, drop enough batter in the skillet to suit the size you would like. As the tops set a bit and show some small bubbles, turn to cook the other side. You may need to add a bit more butter to grease the skillet between batches.

For blueberry pancakes, just drop a few of the berries on the pancakes right before you flip them. If they are frozen, let them thaw before using or you will have little pockets of uncooked dough.

As with the waffles, the leftovers can be frozen and warmed in the toaster or in a 200 oven.

Blueberry Muffins

You Will Need:

2½ cups flour

½ cup sugar

1 tablespoon baking powder

¼ teaspoon baking soda

Pinch of salt

2 eggs

¼ cup melted butter

Scant cup of buttermilk.

1¼ cups blueberries

3 tablespoons sugar mixed with ¼ teaspoon cinnamon

In a large bowl, combine flour, sugar, baking powder, baking soda and salt. In another bowl stir together eggs, melted butter and buttermilk. Add egg mixture to flour and stir until incorporated but don't overdo it. Muffin batter does not need to be smooth. Fold in blueberries.

Grease a muffin tin and scoop batter to ⅔ full in each cup. Sprinkle a bit of cinnamon sugar over the top of each one. You'll get about 10 muffins. Bake at 375 for 20-25 minutes. Turn pan around once so that they brown evenly.

Note:

I have found that muffins and cupcakes cook unevenly and the bottoms may burn when using the tins that have a non-stick coating. I purchased some heavy duty aluminum tins at a restaurant supply store. They are a bit expensive but definitely worth the price.

Paper liners that work well for cupcakes do not peel off easily with muffins. However, I do use the liners to hold the muffins for serving. They look prettier that way and are more tidy for the guests to pick up.

Jammers

The texture of these is pretty similar to the texture of scones. I like them fresh from the oven so I cut the recipe in half if I just want a few for our breakfast.

You Will Need:

2 cups flour

2 tablespoons sugar

1½ teaspoons baking powder

½ teaspoon baking soda

½ teaspoon salt

½ cup cold butter, cut into small pieces

Scant cup of buttermilk

¾ cup of jam (berry or your choice)

In a mixing bowl combine flour, sugar, baking powder, baking soda and salt. Place bowl in the freezer for at least an hour. Remove from freezer, add the cold butter and cut in with a pastry blender or with your food processor. The mixture should be like coarse meal when you are done. Add a scant cup of buttermilk and mix just until clumps form. Turn the dough out onto a floured board and work it a little until it comes together. Do not knead. Pat to a 1" thickness and cut into 2½" rounds. Place on an ungreased cookie sheet and with your thumb make an indentation in each biscuit. Work this around so that the hole is about 1" across. Spoon a generous tablespoon of jam into indentation and bake in 375 oven for about 20–25 minutes.

You should get 6 or 7 biscuits. Serve warm.

Southern Buttermilk Biscuits

These biscuits are good for breakfast or at any time. I use them as a topping for the chicken pot pie that is in the Entrée section of this book.

You Will Need:

2 cups flour

¼ teaspoon baking soda

1 tablespoon baking powder

1 teaspoon salt

6 tablespoons cold shortening (I use butter flavor Crisco)

¾ cup buttermilk

Mix together flour, baking soda, baking powder and salt. Cut in cold shortening until mixture is like coarse meal. Add buttermilk and mix lightly but thoroughly. Knead a few times, just enough to hold the dough together.

Wrap in plastic and refrigerate for 30 minutes.

Pat dough to ½" thick and cut out rounds. Bake 10-12 minutes at 450 until golden.

French Toast

Note:

You can use half and half if you are concerned about the heavy cream. Myself, I go with the cream.

Unfortunately, the best French toast is the one with highest fat content! That is true for a lot of things and this is no exception. It's the heavy cream that really makes the difference.

You Will Need:

4 slices of firm textured bread, slightly stale and cut ½ inch thick

4 large eggs

1 cup heavy cream

Vanilla extract and a bit of cinnamon to taste

4 tablespoons butter

2 tablespoons canola oil

Whisk together the eggs, cream, vanilla and cinnamon. Slice the bread and arrange the slices in one layer in a shallow casserole dish. Pour egg mixture over top and let it soak in for 5minutes. Turn slices over and leave it for another 5 minutes.

In a large skillet start with 2 tablespoons butter and 1 tablespoon Canola oil (oil will keep butter from burning). Melt this over medium heat and when butter is bubbling a bit place several slices of bread in pan. Cook each side over medium heat until golden brown. You will have to add more butter and oil as you continue browning the slices. Place finished pieces on cake racks set on a large cookie sheet in a 200 degree oven. When all slices are done, serve with syrup or sifted powdered sugar and an assortment of berries.

Blintzes

There are many recipes for blintzes and they do not vary much. I have used this one for years and it is very good.

You Will Need:

6 eggs

3 cups flour

1½ teaspoons salt

4 tablespoons melted butter or margarine

1½ cups water

1½ cups milk

For Filling:

3 pounds ricotta or 2 pounds ricotta and 1 pound small curd cottage cheese, well drained

3 large eggs

3 tablespoons sugar

Pinch of salt

2-4 tablespoons unsalted butter for sautéing.

In mixer, beat egg and then gradually add flour, salt and melted butter. Combine milk and water add to flour mixture about a half cup at a time.. Let crepe mixture sit for about an hour or so that the ingredients become homogenized. The batter will also thicken up a bit.

Use an 8 inch skillet with non-stick coating or one that is lightly greased with butter. Over medium heat pour a scant ⅓ cup of batter into skillet and then quickly swirl the pan to make a very thin pancake. Cook on one side only until there are no wet spots on batter. Remove to a flat surface and, when they cool, you may stack them and cover loosely with plastic wrap until ready to fill.

Filling: Combine ricotta and cottage cheese. Add eggs, sugar and salt. Fill crepes on cooked side using 2 tablespoons for each. Place filling in

Note:

I have a wonderful copper skillet that is lined with stainless steel and it is perfect for crepes. I don't often use the coated cookware but I would recommend it for crepes if you can't find an alternative.

center of crepe and fold in 2 sides, then roll the other sides to form a little package.

At this point the blintzes may be frozen. Set them on waxed paper on a cookie sheet and freeze just until hard. Then put them in a ziploc bag and return to the freezer. Let them thaw almost all the way before using. The blintzes may also be assembled and refrigerated the night before serving.

To serve melt 2 tablespoons of butter in a skillet and sauté over medium low heat on both sides until golden brown. Serve with a dollop of sour cream and a spoonful of berry preserves or fresh berries on top.

Yeast Breads

Working with yeast breads can be a very satisfying way to spend a few hours in the kitchen. Using a living organism—yeast—and adding it to other ingredients that you can knead and shape with your hands is magical. The dough rises and bakes and fills your house with such a comforting aroma. There is nothing like it.

Yeast is almost always sold in the dry granulated form as opposed to the compressed refrigerated cakes. When you buy it, be sure the "use by" date is at least 6 months away. One envelope of dry yeast measures out to a scant tablespoon, a helpful thing to know if you are buying it by the jar. In order to activate it, yeast needs to have moisture, a bit of sugar or starch and warmth. The way to find out if your yeast is going to do the job of leavening your bread or rolls is to proof it.

Pour the amount of warm water that is specified in your recipe into a warmed bowl that has enough room for the yeast to rise. The temperature should be between 75 and 85 degrees. An easy way to do this is to run the water onto the inside of your wrist and if it is comfortably warm it will be fine. Sprinkle the yeast onto the surface of the water along with ¼ teaspoon of sugar. Stir it just to combine and set it aside for 10–15 minutes. If it is working the yeast mixture will grow a spongy looking top. If that doesn't happen throw it out and start again. This is called proofing because it proves that your bread will rise properly.

Follow your recipe and, after the ingredients are well combined, knead the dough for about 15 minutes. Push on the dough away from you with the heels of your hands, fold it and give it a quarter turn. Keep on kneading and turning until the dough is smooth. It's good exercise.

When you are ready for the dough to rise, place it in a slightly oiled bowl that will leave room for it to rise to more than double in size. Set it in a warm place, but not close to a heating vent or a hot spot. Don't rush the process. Some breads that are dense can take two hours to rise and other recipes that use more yeast and are "fluffy" can rise in 30–40 minutes. If the instructions say to do a second rising, do it.

Sometimes new cooks are under the impression that using yeast is a complicated thing to do. I always urge people to try it with a basic recipe, maybe one for a simple loaf of white bread. Whether it turns out great or not so great, it's a learning experience and your second try will be better.

Country Crust Bread

This is just a simple recipe that results in 2 basic loaves that are perfect for sandwiches and toast. When it is a bit stale I cut it into cubes to make croutons that are much better than the store bought ones. There is a recipe that I think you will enjoy in the Salad section of this book. I also use the stale slices for the French Toast recipe.

You Will Need:

2 packages or 2 tablespoons dry yeast

2 cups warm water

3 tablespoons sugar

1½ teaspoons salt

2 large eggs

¼ cup vegetable or canola oil

6 cups all purpose flour

In a large mixer bowl dissolve yeast in warm water with a bit of the sugar to be sure the yeast is working. When the mixture expands add the remaining sugar, salt, eggs and oil. Mix this together and then add 3 cups of the flour. Beat until smooth and add enough of the remaining flour until the dough holds together and can be turned out onto a floured board for kneading. Dust with flour and knead until smooth and elastic for about 10 minutes. Place the dough in an oiled bowl, turn it once so that it is oiled on top, cover and allow to rise until doubled. The dough can be refrigerated and set out to raise when needed.

Punch dough down and divide in half. Form into oblongs and place in two 9"x5"x3" loaf pans. Brush with oil and allow to rise until doubled. Bake in a 375 oven for 30–35 minutes. Remove to racks and after 5–10 minutes, remove the loaves from the pans and lay them on their sides on racks.

Semolina Bread

Semolina flour is a golden colored hard wheat product that has a more coarse texture than all purpose flour. It is used in combination with all purpose flour to achieve a loaf with a bit of extra crunch. If you don't plan to use it often I suggest you buy what you need in the bulk foods section of your grocery store.

This recipe is extremely easy and the prep is very fast. The rising time is longer than some recipes so you may want to make it when you are spending the day at home. Don't rush the process.

You Will Need:

1 tablespoon dry yeast

2 cups warm water

½ teaspoon sugar

2½ cups semolina flour

2-3 cups all-purpose flour

2 teaspoons salt

1 egg, beaten with a little cold water

Poppy seeds or sesame seeds, optional

Preheat oven to 425.

Pour warm water into a large mixing bowl and stir in dry yeast and sugar to proof. Let stand 10 minutes until it is bubbly. Add the semolina flour and salt and stir well. Add 2 cups all-purpose flour to make a sticky dough that will come out of the bowl easily. Let it rest a few minutes on a floured board then knead for 10 minutes, adding in another cup or more of the all purpose flour until the dough is smooth and elastic.

Place the dough in an oiled bowl, turn so the top is oiled and cover with a towel. Let rise until triple in size. This will take 2 hours or more. Punch the dough down and cut into two pieces. Shape each piece into a baguette and set the loaves on a large baking sheet that has been oiled and sprinkled with cornmeal. Let rise until almost double and brush with egg wash. Sprinkle with seeds if desired. Slash diagonally on top and slide onto middle rack of oven. Immediately reduce oven to 375 and bake for 30–40 minutes.

NOTE:

I have the double French bread pans which work well. They hold the sides up so that the loaves don't spread out and are more rounded.

Quicky Sticky Buns

This recipe—and the great name for it—came from a book that I bought for $1.79 in 1981 at a grocery store checkout counter. It was one of the best purchases I ever made – ask anyone who has ever eaten one of these yummy treats.

You Will Need:

1¼ cups milk, whole or 2%

¼ cup butter

3½ cups flour

¼ cup sugar

1 egg

1 teaspoon salt

2 scant tablespoons or 2 packets of dry yeast

For Topping:

1 cup packed brown sugar

1 teaspoon cinnamon

½ cup butter

2 tablespoons light corn syrup

1¼ cup coarsely chopped walnuts or pecans

Heat milk with butter until very warm but not hot. In large mixer bowl, combine 2 cups of the flour, the sugar, egg, salt and dry yeast. Slowly pour in the warm milk mixture and, when incorporated, beat for 4 minutes at medium speed. Stir in the remaining 1½ cups flour to form a stiff batter. If your mixer won't handle it, you can do this step by hand. Cover loosely and let rise until doubled. This will take less than an hour because of the relatively large amount of yeast.

While you are waiting for the dough to rise combine the brown sugar, cinnamon, butter, corn syrup and nuts in a medium sized pot. Heat the mixture almost to boiling so that the ingredients are well mixed.

Grease 18 muffin cups and spoon some of the topping mixture in each well. Stir down the batter and drop a generous spoonful of batter onto the topping. A small ice cream scoop works well if it has a release mechanism. Let rise until doubled—20-30 minutes.

Place muffin tins on jelly roll pans to catch any overflow of syrup. Bake at 375 for 15-18 minutes until golden brown. Cool for just a minute, place another cookie sheet on top and invert. Wait a second to let all of the topping settle onto the muffin and lift the tin from the sticky buns. Arrange on a platter and serve.

Note:

The buns freeze well. A gallon zip bag will hold nine of them in three rows. For serving, just wrap what you need in foil and heat in a 300 oven.

Cinnamon Rolls

Note:

At Christmas, I cut the baked rolls into four batches of 6 rolls each and package them for gifts. I include a small container of frosting so that people can warm up the rolls and then frost them. If you are freezing them for later use, do not frost first.

For 18 years, three times a year, the Emerald Empire Kiwanis Club has been picking up litter on a one to two mile stretch of the Beltline Highway here in Eugene. The trash that people throw from their cars, on just this section of roadway, fills each time about 20 of the 33 gallon yellow bags, not including the occasional mattress or broken piece of furniture.

For eleven years Jim was in charge and he decided that it would be a bit of a reward if we provided a brunch at a parking area close to the road. There were usually around 10-12 members signed up to help and we set up a table with food such as fruit, quiche, cheese and crackers, veggies, juices and, most popular of all, two dozen freshly baked cinnamon rolls. I learned soon enough that, if I substituted a different dessert, we were risking a mutiny.

This recipe makes two dozen tender and delicious rolls. The magic ingredient is a 3½ ounce package of vanilla instant pudding. If that doesn't sound good, try this anyway. You will be in for a nice surprise. And you will get rave reviews.

You Will Need:

2 packages or 2 tablespoons dry yeast

½ cup warm water

2 tablespoons sugar

3½ ounce package of vanilla instant pudding

2 cups whole or 2% milk

½ cup melted margarine

2 large eggs, beaten

1½ teaspoons salt

8 cups flour

Filling:

½-¾ cup melted butter

2 cups packed brown sugar, mixed with 4 teaspoons cinnamon

Frosting:

4 tablespoons softened butter

1 teaspoon vanilla

1½ cups powdered sugar

Small amount of milk to make a thin icing for drizzling over rolls

In a small bowl, combine warm water and yeast and sugar. Stir until dissolved. In a very large bowl, mix pudding with the milk according to package directions. Add margarine, eggs and salt. Add yeast mixture and mix well. Gradually add flour, turning out onto a board when it begins to hold together, usually after about 6 cups have been added. Knead until smooth.

The dough can be used right away or refrigerated overnight and brought to room temperature when ready to use. Cover and let rise until doubled.

When ready to form, punch the dough down and divide it in half. Roll each piece into a rectangle about 14x18". Brush each with half of melted butter and half of the sugar mix. Roll up dough from the long end and cut in 12 pieces. This can be done with a piece of heavy thread, sliding it under the roll and crossing it to tighten and cut. Or, if you have a very sharp knife, just brush a little flour on it so it won't stick to the dough. To keep the pieces uniform in size cut the roll in half and then into quarters and each quarter into three pieces.

Place 12 rolls evenly spaced, in each of two greased 9x13" pans, pressing each roll down slightly. Cover and let rise until double. Bake at 350 for about 20 minutes until nicely golden but not brown. Remove from oven and loosen around edges. Place a cookie sheet over top and turn rolls out on it. Transfer to a rack to cool.

When almost cool drizzle with frosting which is made by combining the butter, vanilla and powdered sugar and thinning it with the milk.

Butter Coffeecakes With Streusel Topping

This recipe makes three beautiful and delicious coffeecakes, the texture being the same as a croissant. If you are not using all three the others will freeze well.

You Will Need:

½ cup warm water

2 packages or two scant tablespoons yeast

1 cup milk, scalded and cooled to lukewarm

⅓ cup sugar

1½ teaspoons salt

2 large eggs

1 teaspoon vanilla

5 cups flour

2 sticks unsalted butter

Pecan halves

1 egg yolk, beaten with 2 tablespoons milk

½ stick butter

½ cup flour

½ cup packed brown sugar

1 teaspoon cinnamon

1 cup powdered sugar

Milk, enough to thin the powdered sugar

Place warm water in a large bowl, swirl it around to warm the bowl and pour it out. Add the ½ cup of warm water to the bowl and sprinkle the yeast over the top of it. Stir a tablespoon of the sugar into the yeast and allow it to sit about 10 minutes until the mixture foams. Add the warm milk, the rest of the sugar, salt, eggs and vanilla.

Gradually add 3½ cups flour and stir it to make a soft dough. Spread ½ cup of flour on a board or work surface and turn out the dough. Begin kneading the dough while adding enough of the last cup of flour until it is smooth and elastic.

Flour the board a little and roll out the dough to a 12x18" rectangle. Cut 1/3 of the cold butter into small pieces and scatter them on two thirds of the dough leaving a small border. Fold the portion of dough that is not covered with butter over onto the middle section and then fold it once more to cover the last third. Pinch the edges to seal and flour the board and roll the dough again to 12x18". Repeat the buttering and folding process and then do the whole thing once more.

Refrigerate the dough, wrapped tightly, overnight.

The next day, unwrap the dough and cut it into three sections, one for each coffeecake. Cut each section into three strips and roll each strip into a 28" rope. Don't flour your work surface at this stage. Braid the ropes and pinch the ends to seal. Place braid in a greased 9" cake pan, coiling it around outside edge and proceed into the center. Tuck pecan halves into the ropes and brush the top of the braid with the egg wash.

Lightly press streusel topping on top.

Repeat this process for the other two cakes and let them rise in a warm place for an hour or until almost doubled.

Bake in a 375 oven for 30 minutes or until golden brown. Cool in pans for 10 minutes and carefully loosen them around the edges and remove with a large spatula to racks.

While still slightly warm, drizzle with powdered sugar that has been mixed with a small amount of milk to allow it to pour from a spoon.

Cottage Cheese Rolls

Although this recipe calls for yeast it does not require a long rising process. The rolls are very quick to prepare and are not overly sweet.

You Will Need:

1 package or 1 scant tablespoon yeast

¼ cup warm water

A pinch of sugar

2½ cups flour

¼ cup sugar

¾ teaspoon salt

1 stick cold unsalted butter

1½ cups cottage cheese

1 large egg, beaten

6 tablespoons softened butter

¾ cup brown sugar

½ teaspoon cinnamon

¼ cup finely chopped walnuts

Dissolve yeast in warm water and add a pinch of sugar to make sure the yeast is working.

In a large mixing bowl mix together the flour, sugar, and salt. Cut in the stick of cold butter and work it into the dough as you would a pie crust dough until it resembles cornmeal. Add the cottage cheese, egg and yeast mixture and form the dough into a ball. Let it sit for 10 minutes.

In a separate bowl combine the softened butter, brown sugar, cinnamon and walnuts until it is spreadable.

Roll out the dough on a floured surface until it measures about 12x14 inches. Drop teaspoons of filling all along the rectangle and then very gently spread it. Roll dough up from the 14" side and then cut it into

12 slices. This is more easily done with this sticky dough by sliding a long piece of heavy thread under the roll until it reaches the middle. Crisscross the thread over the top and pull it until the roll is cut. To get slices of the same width cut each half in half and each piece into three slices.

Place the rolls on two lightly greased baking sheets and cover lightly with a thin towel. When doubled in size bake at 350 for about 20 minutes. When they are lightly brown, remove from oven and let them set for a few minutes. Remove to a cooling rack.

Vienna Brioche Loaf

You Will Need:

1 package or 1 scant tablespoon dry yeast

½ cup warm water

A pinch of sugar

1 cup softened butter

¼ cup sugar

1 teaspoon salt

1 teaspoon lemon zest (optional)

6 large eggs

4½ cups flour

Filling:

3 tablespoons softened butter

⅔ cup brown sugar

2 egg yolks

2 tablespoons whole milk

½ teaspoon vanilla

2 cups finely chopped nuts (I use walnuts)

Dissolve yeast in the warm water. Sprinkle a little sugar in to proof.

In large bowl of mixer, beat softened butter with sugar, salt and lemon zest. Add yeast and mix in. Beat in eggs and 3 cups of the flour and continue mixing for 4 minutes. Add remaining 1½ cups flour at low speed. Cover bowl and let rise for 2 hours, then refrigerate overnight. Next morning combine filling ingredients and stir down the dough – it will be soft. Cut in half and roll each half on a floured board into a 9x13 rectangle. Brush with melted butter and spread with filling to ½ inch of edges. Roll up from each 9" edge toward center. Place each in loaf in an oiled 9x5x3 loaf pan. Brush with melted butter and let rise until double. Bake at 350 – 35 minutes. Remove to racks to cool and then sift powdered sugar over the top.

BAKING WITH THE KIDDOS

Our three girls were born between 1965 and 1968 and Jim and I have always believed they are the crowning glory of our lives. They are that great.

However, even I, the person who would throw myself in front of a bus for them and therefore leave them guilt ridden for life, had days when I fantasized about driving down the expressway which, by the way, had an on-ramp at the end of our street. It didn't lead to anyplace special, just Northwest, but it was probably quiet there. I could take a few books with me.

Jim was working long hours and spent his time talking to people who could respond intelligibly but not necessarily intelligently. I, on the other hand, was herding my highly intelligent wee ones, who had not all reached the age of reason—it is somewhere around seven, I believe—from one activity to another. On good weather days they ran around in the yard doing whatever nutty games they could think of while I sat on the porch reading or knitting or doing something that didn't involve exercise.

Since we were living in Oregon, the more challenging times were those rainy days when I was open to just about anything. Some options for my girls included cutting up pieces of paper and gluing them onto a bigger piece of paper or doing a rudimentary version of gymnastics on and around the furniture. A very popular game that my clever children thought of was one that began by throwing goldfish crackers onto the kitchen carpet. This made sense because the blue and green industrial carpet kind of looked like water. Their fishing poles were pencils with a string at the end and a paper clip to anchor the string. No way could they land a fish, especially since it was a cracker, but they were happy and since we were never going to take them fishing for real it seemed like a good alternative.

A big asset of our house was our large basement and the girls and their friends were free to run around or roller skate there with the stipulation "Do Not Throw Anything in the Sump Pump or Fall into the Hole".

We did go out to pre-school, play dates, swimming, bike riding and there was always TV, Mr. Rogers being my favorite babysitter.

I was reminiscing and thinking that this made for a pretty fun childhood and so I asked my girls, as adults, what they remembered about me when they were small and they said they just remembered playing with each other. I told them I was re-considering sacrificing myself in the path of the bus. So then they mentioned that they did recall me doing some cooking with them. It is my favorite thing to do and this next recipe was one we did because I thought the magic part would impress them along with the totally sweet and junky nature of it. Starting from there, they progressed far enough in cooking so that, as they got a bit older, they opened the highly successful Cookie Jar Bakery (only two customers, but very devoted ones). They made pies, cookies, and breads, all very fresh on delivery. In August they baked for the County Fair contests for kids and always won ribbons and prize money for their efforts. Amazing kids, right?

Magic Marshmallow Puffs

This may not impress at the gourmet table but it is a hit with the under ten crowd. It is my sentimental favorite.

You Will Need:

2 cans of Pillsbury crescent rolls

⅓ cup sugar

1 teaspoon cinnamon

Large marshmallows

¼ cup butter

1 cup powdered sugar

A bit of milk

Separate the triangles of the crescent rolls. Mix together the sugar and cinnamon. Sprinkle some of this on each triangle, place a large marshmallow on top of sugar and, starting at the pointed end, roll the dough around the marshmallow so it is completely covered. Pinch dough together so that it is sealed well.

Melt butter and roll each dough ball in it and place it in greased muffin tins.

Bake at 375 until golden.

Remove from tins onto rack and let cool a bit. Then drizzle with powdered sugar that has been mixed with a little milk.

The marshmallow disappears—it's magic! And the puffs soon disappear too.

Zucchini Bread

When I had my own garden, I always had plenty of zucchini. Too much, in fact, because I could never get myself to plant just one. Even though I haven't had a garden for many years, I haven't missed a summer without someone giving me zucchini. It's one of those crazy little constants in life and I would miss it if it didn't happen.

This recipe makes two very flavorful and moist loaves.

You will Need:

3 large eggs

1 cup vegetable oil

1½ cups sugar

2 teaspoons vanilla

2 cups coarsely shredded zucchini

1 8-ounce can crushed pineapple, well drained

3 cups flour

2 teaspoons baking soda

1 teaspoon salt

1 teaspoon baking powder

1½ teaspoons cinnamon

¾ teaspoon nutmeg

1 cup chopped walnuts

In the large bowl of a mixer, cream together eggs, oil, sugar and vanilla. Add 2 cups coarsely shredded zucchini and pineapple and mix to incorporate it.

In a smaller bowl, combine flour, baking soda, salt, baking powder, cinnamon, nutmeg and nuts. Stir this into zucchini mixture just until blended. Divide into 2 loaf pans that have been oiled and coated with sugar. Bake at 350 for about 50-60 minutes. Remove from oven and cool a few minutes and turn out on racks.

Note:

These can also be baked in 4 baby loaf pans for gift giving. Check after 40-45 minutes. Cool the loaves, wrap them well and freeze.

Blueberry Crumb Cake

This is a pretty traditional coffeecake that is enhanced by the addition of blueberries – any variety will do.

You Will Need:

2 cups blueberries, washed and dried

2 cups flour

2 teaspoons baking powder

½ teaspoon salt

¼ cup butter

¾ cup sugar

1 teaspoon vanilla

1 large egg

½ cup whole milk

A few tablespoons dry bread crumbs

½ cup finely chopped walnuts

For the Topping:

⅓ cup flour

½ cup sugar

1 teaspoon cinnamon

¼ cup butter

Butter a 9" square pan and dust it with the dry bread crumbs.

In a small bowl, combine the topping ingredients, cutting in the butter until it is crumbly. Set aside.

Combine the 2 cups flour, baking powder and salt in another bowl. Place blueberries in a separate bowl and sprinkle them with 2 tablespoons of the flour mixture. Set the berries aside.

In large mixer bowl cream ¼ cup butter with ¾ cup sugar. Beat in egg until light and fluffy and then beat in vanilla. Stir in flour mixture alternately with milk. Fold in blueberries.

Turn the batter into the prepared pan being careful to not disturb the bread crumbs. The batter is stiff so you can drop spoonfuls of it into the pan and then carefully spread it. Sprinkle with the chopped nuts and then with the crumb topping.

Bake at 375 for 50 minutes or until a tester comes out clean. Cool on a rack for 30 minutes.

Loosen around the edges and place a large flat plate on top. Turn cake out and then place your serving dish on the bottom of the cake and invert again.

If you would like, you could sift some powdered sugar on top of the cake and scatter some blueberries around the plate.

LIFE AS IT IS

I met Mary Hoxie when I was hired to be Director of Local Aid, a non-profit that was established to assist low income families in Junction City with essentials such as food boxes, energy payments and prescriptions. Mary had been working there for years helping previous directors, and she told me later that she and the other volunteers thought I had been hired because I was friends with Robin who was one of the Board Members. That probably helped although I did have some experience running a Soup Kitchen and serving on Boards of other non-profits. My new job would involve running an agency that served over 200 families a month, the equivalent of 660 people, a much bigger challenge.

As I became more settled in my job I realized that we could do some things that would be a real benefit to the children we served. The Board agreed and we provided the schools with boxes of lice treatment so that families would get an immediate fix for the problem. We bought bike helmets that the kids proudly wore in the Pet Parade, and, most importantly, we paid for emergency dental care for children in extreme pain who were referred to the school nurse. These programs were a success and were funded mostly by a very generous community.

I had a variety of jobs in my life. They were experiences I value, for what I learned and the people I met. Local Aid was the one that had the most impact in my life. I learned close up about the struggles of our clients who were trying hard to usher their families through difficult times. It was important to help them do that. I accepted all invitations to speak to civic groups or church congregations. It was a chance to explain the plight of the poor and also to make a plea for funding. Inevitably someone would ask about the "bad apples" who were coming in for food and other help, and I needed to gently remind my audience that there could be a few of those apples in any kind of group, but you have to keep the focus on your underlying mission.

I felt privileged that I had the opportunity to listen to the stories of the clients. My office became a place where I could hear about their lives, interesting, sad, filled with bad decisions and often just unfortunate circumstances beyond their ability to control. I received gifts of cookies, chicken mole, cards with sweet notes and hugs from the little ones. I can still see their faces and hear the things they taught me. I am in their debt.

Plum Kuchen

The plums in this recipe and in the tart recipe elsewhere in this book are a real snap to make because of the bags of sliced plums, courtesy of Mary, that are in my freezer. Plums aside, she is generous beyond belief and an amazing friend.

You Will Need:

3 tablespoons flour

1½ tablespoons sugar

1½ tablespoons butter

1½ cups flour

¾ cup sugar

2 teaspoons baking powder

¼ teaspoon salt

1 large egg

½ cup milk

¼ cup Canola or vegetable oil

4 medium plums cut into slices

Make the topping by combining the 3 tablespoons flour and 1½ table-spoons sugar. Cut in the butter until the mixture is like coarse crumbs. Set aside.

In another bowl stir together the flour, sugar, baking powder and salt. Combine the egg, milk and oil in another bowl. Make a well in the dry ingredients and pour the egg mixture into it. Stir just until the batter is moistened and a bit lumpy.

Spread batter into a greased and floured 11 inch flan pan with a remov-able bottom. Arrange plum slices on top in an attractive pattern. Sprinkle with topping. Bake at 375 for 30–35 minutes.

Desserts

A BIT ABOUT BAKING

Baking recipes, even if not specified, always call for unsalted butter. If you only have salted butter I suggest you cut the amount of salt in the recipe in half.

If a recipe calls for milk it means whole milk unless otherwise noted. You may be able to substitute 2% but skim or 1% will alter the fat content and that is what contributes to the tenderness of your finished product. If a recipe calls for cream or half and half instead of milk there is a reason for it.

Eggs that are called for in baking are always large unless otherwise stated. It is helpful to know that a large egg measures out to 3 tablespoons and a large egg white to 2 tablespoons. I sometimes get cartons of fresh out of the coop eggs from a friend and they contain an assortment of sizes. I can figure out the equivalent of 2 large eggs by filling my measuring cup to the 6 tablespoon line. And when I need to brush a shiny top on a loaf of bread or something else I can use up one of the banty eggs.

NEVER buy artificial extracts. I know the real thing can be more expensive but there really is no substitute. You don't have to buy the super gourmet ones that are imported from remote gathering places and cost more than your shoes. Just look for the word PURE on the label. You may notice that the ingredients listed include water or alcohol or both. That is because they are part of the extraction process.

A friend of mine used anise oil in a recipe I had given her, substituting it for extract teaspoon for teaspoon. As I walked down our driveway I could smell the loaf she sent me, tightly wrapped and sitting in my closed mailbox. Even though the bread was inedible I admired the braiding and I loved the note she sent that said how proud she was that she made it.

There are a few things you can do to give yourself a head start on your baking. I make up a small jar of cinnamon sugar – a cup of sugar to a ½ teaspoon or more of cinnamon. It is something I use often for sprinkling on biscotti or pie crust or for just making cinnamon toast. If you have a combo that you use frequently such as the spices in the pumpkin cheesecake or the gingerbread, measure them into a small jar to save time later. If you make a lot of cheesecakes, buy the large sized box of graham crackers and crush enough of them to store several plastic bags holding 2 cups of crumbs. They will keep for a month in your pantry or in your freezer for a longer time and you will only have to wash your food processor once.

An offset spatula is the essential tool for evenly smoothing the batter in your cake pan before baking. You can find them in many sizes but my favorite is a little inexpensive one with a blade that is ¾" wide and about 4" long. It is bent at the handle – offset. You'll be surprised at how slick this is. If you are preparing cakes in large sheet sized pans a large offset is helpful and it is also handy for smoothing frosting on the sides of a layer cake.

I have two sizes of ice cream scoops—one large that works perfectly for filling muffin or cupcake tins and a smaller one that I use for cookie dough. You want to buy the scoops that have the mechanism that will plop the dough out and onto the baking sheet. Your cookies or muffins will all be the same size.

I highly recommend a book called The Food Lover's Companion by Sharon and Ron Herbst. I have never failed to find an answer to my cooking questions in it.

I never use the non-stick coated baking pans. My experience with them has been that the cakes, cupcakes or cookies burn on the bottom. I have some wonderful sturdy commercial tins and pans that cook very evenly. The best place to look for these is at a restaurant supply store.

For baking pies, I could not get along without my 12" round metal pan with a very low fluted edge which I have had forever. It has a 3½" wide hole in the center which I believe provides for more even baking. The perimeter keeps any overflow of pie juices from making a mess of your oven. Your pie plate will sit up a bit over the center hole of the pan so it would not work for tart pans with removable bottoms. Those should sit very flat on your oven racks or on a cookie sheet.

If you don't have a French rolling pin for making pie crusts, try one. Mine is 19" long and is 4½" in circumference at the middle and 3½" circumference at the ends. I don't know the dynamics of it but it makes the process faster and easier. Many professional chefs recommend these and, if you try one, you will see why.

One of the things that is essential to my kitchen is my scale. Here is why I love it. When I need two layers for a cake, I want them to be the same thickness. I fill two cake pans and then I weigh each one. If there is a discrepancy in the weights I transfer some batter so that they are equal. When I make biscotti, the dough must be divided into thirds that I roll into logs to fit onto my long baking sheet. The same is true for bread that is split for two baguettes. You really will end up with a more attractive and consistent product.

COOKIES, BEVERLY AND LIFE LESSONS

Until I was in 7th grade we lived in a house that was just three doors away from our parish school, St. Anthony's. It was in a working class neighborhood, a mostly Italian one although there were a few Polish and Irish families there too. My best friend Beverly lived directly across the street where the houses were perched atop a hill and, to reach the front door, you had to trek up twenty or so steps.

Beverly and I made a good pair. We were both easy going and quiet and although I didn't know how we could be "our own grandmas", that is what my mother called us. We played the games of kids of the fifties, roller skating, coloring, riding bikes or hanging out at the summer camp at the park. We sometimes walked to the end of our street and made our way up the wooden stairs that had been built there, many years earlier, as a short cut to the street above. As people began driving more the stairs were rarely used so they were perfect for us to sit on and exchange bits of information that we thought would be a revelation to the other person. Beverly won the prize for what I considered the craziest story I had ever heard, the one about how a man and a woman came together in a very preposterous way and then a good while later a baby came out. My nine year old self didn't believe a word of it and since I would not be getting that information at my Catholic school or from my parents, my only recourse much later was to look through my dad's medical books when no one was home. And that I did.

Some of our time was spent in the kitchen at Beverly's house where her mother, Jenny, was frequently baking. We just hung out at the table so that we could lick the beaters and wait for whatever was coming out of the oven. And everything else aside, it was a chance to be with Jenny, the sweetest woman around.

I do know for sure that cookies are a gift, whether you give or receive them so I hope you will try some of the following recipes. They will make someone smile.

Cranberry-Almond Biscotti

Note:

I am beginning this chapter with what I think may be the most well known treat in the repertoire of Italian baking. Biscotti are almost always a twice baked cookie or biscuit. Once you master the technique you will be able to prepare many variations of them. The following recipes are my favorites and I think they are easy beginner ones.

There are often recipes that come from different cultural traditions that are very similar. I developed this biscotti from a recipe for Mandelbrot given to me by a Jewish friend, Elaine, in the late 1960's. I added the cranberries and orange zest for more flavor and the cinnamon sugar for a bit of sweetness on top. You will find that the texture of these is lighter than the ones you may buy at the market but they are still great for dunking in your coffee. Among friends and family they are the most favorite of my biscotti.

You Will Need:

4 large eggs

1 cup sugar

1 cup vegetable or canola oil

1 teaspoon almond extract

2 teaspoons vanilla extract

Finely grated zest of one orange, optional

4 cups flour

½ teaspoon baking soda

1 tablespoon baking powder

1 cup dried cranberries

1 cup slivered almonds

Canola oil for brushing on loaves

¼ cup sugar mixed with a little cinnamon

In a large mixer bowl, beat eggs, sugar and vegetable oil until well blended. Mix in orange zest, almond extract and vanilla. In another bowl, combine flour, baking soda and baking powder. Blend half of this mixture into the beaten eggs and then add the dried cranberries and slivered almonds. Add the remaining flour and mix just until blended. Turn onto a lightly floured board and knead just enough so that it is not sticky and is well combined. You may need to use a bit more flour on it while kneading. Cut into three equal pieces and roll each piece into a log about 12-14 inches long. Place these on a lightly greased 11x15" baking pan. Brush oil on top of each loaf and sprinkle with the cinnamon sugar. Bake at 350 for about 30 minutes or until lightly browned. Test with a wooden skewer to be sure that the loaves are cooked through.

Let the loaves cool and then slice them on the diagonal at almost ½ inch intervals. Lay the pieces on a baking sheet and toast in a 375 oven for about 8 minutes or until lightly golden. You may need to turn them over once during this process so that they are evenly toasted. Cool biscotti on racks and then store them in a tightly covered container. They will keep for several weeks.

Note:

You can make party favors or just a nice little gift by wrapping six or eight of these biscotti in cellophane and tying them up with a pretty ribbon. At Christmastime I give tins of them as gifts. It beats fighting the crowds at the mall and my friends look forward to getting them.

Cinnamon Date Nut Biscotti

Note:

Instead of slicing all of these, wrap the whole logs you are not using in foil and slice as needed. They stay fresher that way. Also, if you just want a few dozen biscotti, the ingredients in this recipe can easily be cut in half.

These biscotti can be made very quickly since they do not have to be toasted after slicing. They are the exception to the rule of twice baked and are a bit chewy instead of crispy. Very tasty though.

You Will Need:

4 cups flour

1 teaspoon cinnamon

1 teaspoon baking soda

1 cup chopped walnuts

1 cup chopped dates

4 large eggs, beaten

1 cup vegetable oil

1 cup sugar

1 cup brown sugar

¼ cup sugar mixed with ¼ teaspoon cinnamon (optional)

In a large bowl, combine flour, cinnamon, baking soda, walnuts and dates.

In a smaller bowl, combine eggs, oil, sugar and brown sugar.

Form a well in the dry mixture and pour the egg mixture into it. Mix until combined and turn out onto a lightly floured board. Knead for a few minutes until blended. If the dough is too sticky add a little more flour.

Lightly grease or line a large baking sheet with parchment paper. Divide the dough into four equal pieces and form each into a log about 12" long. These will fit crosswise on an extra large jelly roll pan or you could bake two at a time on a regular sized one. Brush logs with a little oil and sprinkle with sugar mixture.

Bake for 20-25 minutes in a 350 oven until tester comes out clean. Cool on wire racks then slice diagonally into ½ inch pieces.

Coconut Almond Biscotti Dipped in Chocolate

I usually make this biscotti as an addition to a tray of other varieties. Not everyone likes coconut but, for those of us who do, this is a delicious treat.

You Will Need:

½ cup softened unsalted butter

1 cup sugar

2 large eggs

¾ teaspoon almond extract

2 teaspoons vanilla

1¼ cups sweetened shredded coconut

¾ cup slivered almonds

2 cups flour

1½ teaspoons baking powder

¼ teaspoon salt

Dipping chocolate

In a large mixer bowl, cream butter and sugar, mixing this until very light. Beat in eggs, almond extract and vanilla. Add coconut and almonds. Mix together flour, baking powder and salt and add this gradually to the creamed mixture.

Divide dough into three equal pieces. If it is too sticky, dust with a little flour. Form into logs about 12 inches long and place on a parchment lined baking sheet. Bake at 350 for about 25 minutes. Remove from oven and let cool.

Slice on the diagonal ½ inch thick, place on baking sheet and toast at

If you don't use coconut often, don't forget that you can buy it in the bulk foods section of the market. It is very fresh and you can buy just the amount that you need.

350 for about 10-12 minutes. Watch carefully so they only get to light golden brown.

Cool again on racks and store in airtight containers. If you wish to glaze them, do this when you are ready to serve them or before packaging.

Glaze: Just follow the directions on the dipping chocolate that you purchase. It is not necessary to add anything to the chocolate and usually it does not require tempering. This product works well because it hardens enough for you to store the biscotti or package them for gift giving without the chocolate smearing.

Molasses Cookies

I make these often – and they disappear fast. They smell wonderful when they are baking and I would recommend eating one as soon as it comes out of the oven. They are truly irresistible.

You Will Need:

1 cup plus 3 tablespoons vegetable shortening

1 cup sugar

¼ cup molasses, light or dark depending on your taste

1 large egg

2½ cups flour

2 teaspoons baking soda

1 teaspoon cinnamon

1 teaspoon ginger

½ teaspoon ground cloves

3-4 tablespoons sugar for rolling

In large mixer bowl, beat together vegetable shortening (I use butter flavor Crisco), sugar and molasses. When this is well combined, beat in 1 egg. In a separate bowl mix together flour, baking soda, cinnamon, ginger and ground cloves. Add to mixer bowl in 3 steps, beating well after each addition. Roll into walnut sized balls and roll these in sugar. Transfer to a greased baking sheet and press flat with a glass that is buttered on bottom and dipped in sugar.

Bake at 350 until golden but be careful not to brown too much – around 10-12 minutes. You will have about 4 dozen cookies.

Note:

This dough keeps for a week in the refrigerator and when chilled is easy to work with. However it is not necessary to refrigerate it.

Unbelievable Peanut Butter Cookies

No, I didn't leave anything out. These cookies have only four ingredients and flour is not one of them. They have the texture of shortbread and are very peanut buttery. Quick and easy too.

You Will Need:

1 cup peanut butter, unsweetened

1 cup white sugar

1 large egg

1 teaspoon baking soda

Combine ingredients in your mixer bowl and beat on medium speed until mixture is completely blended and it holds together when you form the dough into balls.

Lightly grease two baking sheets. Make walnut sized balls of dough and place on cookie sheets. Use a fork to make a crisscross pattern as you gently flatten each cookie.

Bake for about 12 minutes in a 350 oven. Let them sit a few minutes before removing to cooling racks so they do not fall apart. Once they are cool, they will hold together fine. You will get about 16 cookies.

Note: To ensure that the cookies are not overly sweet use a brand of peanut butter that has no added sugar.

Very Chocolate Brownies

Brownies are just about the easiest dessert to make and these are no exception. They are very good with or without the walnuts.

You Will Need:

¾ cup flour

¼ teaspoon baking soda

¾ cup sugar

⅓ cup unsalted butter

2 tablespoons water

1¾ cups semisweet chocolate chips

1 teaspoon vanilla

2 large eggs

½ cup chopped walnuts (optional)

In a small saucepan, combine sugar, butter and water. Bring to a boil over medium heat, then remove from heat. Stir in 1 cup of the chocolate chips and vanilla, mix until smooth. Transfer to a bowl that is large enough to accommodate the other ingredients. Cool completely.

When cool, stir in eggs, one at a time, beating well. Mix together the flour and soda and add to chocolate mixture gradually. Beat until smooth then stir in ¾ cup chocolate chips and nuts.

Pour into a greased 9" square pan, even out the batter and bake at 325 for 30-35 minutes. Test to make sure they are completely cooked. Cool on wire rack and then cut into squares.

Note:

You can transform these into an even more special dessert by topping each brownie with a scoop of vanilla ice cream and then drizzling it with caramel sauce. YUMMY!

Melt In Your Mouth Sugar Cookies

Note:

There are no eggs in this recipe but be assured that they hold together well anyway.

This is another cookie with very few ingredients, two of them being butter and margarine. They are very light and delicate.

You Will Need:

½ cup unsalted butter

½ cup margarine

½ cup sugar

1 cup flour

1½ cups quick cooking oats

A little sugar

A little powdered sugar

Beat the butter and margarine with the sugar until light and fluffy. Add the flour and then the oats. That's it. Now shape balls using a heaping teaspoon of batter for each. Place these on parchment covered cookie sheets and gently flatten with the bottom of a glass that has been greased and dipped in sugar. Bake at 350 for 12-15 minutes. Cool on racks and dust with powdered sugar. You will get about 40 cookies.

Oatmeal Cookies

I know that butter and sugar are not the healthiest parts of your diet but we all need a cookie now and then and these compensate by being loaded with oatmeal and raisins (or chocolate chips if you want to go all out).

You Will Need:

1½ sticks unsalted butter, softened

½ cup granulated sugar

1 cup brown sugar

1 large egg

2 tablespoons water

1½ teaspoons vanilla

⅔ cup flour

1 teaspoon cinnamon

½ teaspoon salt

½ teaspoon baking soda

3 cups quick cooking oatmeal

1 cup raisins or 1 cup chocolate chips

Cream the butter, white sugar and brown sugar until fluffy. Beat in egg until well combined then beat in water and vanilla.

In a small bowl stir together the flour, cinnamon, baking soda and salt. Add this to the egg mixture and mix well.

At this time you can stir in raisins or chocolate chips. If you can't decide which one, divide your dough in half and add ½ cup of raisins to one half and ½ cup of chips to the other. Or you could use ½ cup of each in all of the batter.

Form into balls a bit bigger than a golf ball and place on greased cookie sheets. Flatten them slightly and bake at 350 for 18-20 minutes or until edges are lightly brown. Centers will still be soft. Remove from oven and let cool for a few minutes. Remove cookies to wire racks.

Toffee Bars

Our 12 year old grandson Leo has a very popular home business in Portland called Good Stuff. This is one of his delicious offerings.

You Will Need:

2 cups flour

¾ cup cold unsalted butter, cut into small pieces

⅓ cup brown sugar, firmly packed

¼ teaspoon salt

½ cup unsalted butter

¾ cup brown sugar, firmly packed

⅓ cup honey

2 tablespoons milk

2 cups coarsely chopped nuts (walnuts, almonds, pecans or a combination of these)

Cut the ¾ cup butter into the 2 cups flour using a food processor or a pastry blender until there are very tiny pieces of butter throughout. Add the brown sugar and salt. Pulse or mix in by hand. Press mixture into the bottom of a 9x13 ungreased pan. Bake the crust on the middle rack of a 375 oven for 10 minutes, rotate the pan and bake for 5-10 minutes more until golden. Remove from oven and reduce heat to 325 degrees.

While the crust is baking melt the ½ cup butter in a saucepan and then stir in the ¾ cup brown sugar, honey and milk. Cook over medium high heat for a minute or two, until well combined, and stir in nuts. Pour over the hot crumb crust. Bake for 10 minutes in the 325 oven, rotate the pan and bake 5-10 minutes more, until topping bubbles. Cool and cut into bars. Cutting 3 across and 6 down will get you 18 servings.

Lemon Bars

You Will Need:

For the Crust:

½ cup butter

1 cup flour

¼ cup powdered sugar

For the Filling:

1 cup sugar

2 teaspoons lemon zest

2 tablespoons freshly squeezed lemon juice

½ teaspoon baking powder

¼ teaspoon salt

2 large eggs

Powdered sugar for sifting over top

Prepare the crust ingredients as you would for a pie shell, cutting in the butter until it is uniformly distributed. Press the mixture into an ungreased 8x8x2" baking pan. Bake in a 350 oven for 20 minutes.

While the crust is baking beat the sugar, lemon zest and juice, baking powder, salt and 2 eggs for three minutes on high until light and fluffy. Pour over hot crust and return to the oven for 25-30 minutes until filling is firm enough to not leave a dent when touched.

Cool and cut into 16 squares and then sift powdered sugar over the top.

Sour Cream Raisin Bars

One of my volunteers at work brought in a plate of these delicious bars. The recipe is from a very old book that was printed before the days of calculating calories from fat.

You Will Need:

2 cups raisins

1½ cups water

1½ cups flour

1½ cups old fashioned rolled oats (not quick)

1 cup packed brown sugar

1 teaspoon baking soda

¾ cup unsalted butter, softened

1 cup sugar

1 cup sour cream (low fat type works also)

3 large egg yolks

2 tablespoons cornstarch

First, simmer the raisins in water over medium heat until they are soft and plump (about 10 minutes). Drain and cool.

In mixer, combine flour, rolled oats, brown sugar and baking soda. Add butter and beat until incorporated but still crumbly. Press 3 cups of this mixture onto the bottom of a 9x13 ungreased pan.

Filling: In a saucepan, combine sugar, sour cream, egg yolks and cornstarch. Cook over low heat, stirring occasionally until mixture comes to a boil. You may have to turn heat up a little. Boil for 1 minute, remove from heat and stir in raisins. Spoon the filling over the crust and sprinkle with remaining crumbs. Bake at 350 for 25-35 minutes or until top is lightly browned. Cool completely and cut into bars.

Pumpkin Bars

When I was a new bride this recipe was given to me by a really sweet woman named Bubbles. Her name was really Rose but, when my Dad gave her a nickname, she became forever known as Bubbles. At one of our Thanksgiving dinners she brought this dessert and for me it was much better than the usual pie.

It is extremely easy to make.

You Will Need:

4 large eggs

1⅔ cups sugar

1 cup Canola oil

1 16-ounce can of pumpkin

2 cups flour

2 teaspoons baking powder

2 teaspoons cinnamon

1 teaspoon salt

1 teaspoon baking soda

In a large mixer bowl beat together the eggs and sugar and with the mixer running gradually add the oil and the pumpkin and mix until well combined.

In another bowl stir together the remaining ingredients and add them half at a time to the egg mixture. Pour into a 10x15" ungreased baking pan. Bake 25-30 minutes at 350.

Cool in the pan and top with cream cheese frosting – recipe in this book. Cut into squares of any size you desire.

Dozens Of Nut Rolls

These nut rolls are similar to rugalach except that the filling is a simple walnut mixture. The dough is exceptionally rich and tender. The recipe makes 8 dozen but can easily be cut in half.

You Will Need:

4 cups flour

1 pound unsalted butter

2 large eggs, separated

1½ cups sour cream

1½ cups sugar

2 teaspoon cinnamon

1½ cups finely chopped walnuts

For the dough: Measure flour into bowl of your food processor, then add butter, cut up, and pulse as you would pastry dough. You can do this step with a pastry blender if you don't have a food processor. Add egg yolks and sour cream to bowl and process or work in until the mixture holds together. Divide dough into 2 disks and refrigerate these overnight or for several hours. For the Filling: Mix together sugar, cinnamon and walnuts.

To bake, first divide each disk of dough into 4 equal pieces. Wrap and refrigerate the pieces you are not using as you work. Roll each piece on a lightly floured board into a large circle ⅛" inch thick. Beat the egg whites with a little water and brush some of this onto the dough. Then sprinkle with some of the nut mixture. Cut into 12 pie shaped pieces. Roll each piece up from the wide edge and curve the roll into a crescent shape.

Bake on a greased cookie sheet at 350 for 20-25 minutes or until lightly golden on top. Watch them carefully so they don't get too dark.

These will keep for a week or so in a tightly covered container.

PARTY TIME

Since the party was a potluck – my first ever potluck—I decided that my offering would be a chocolate cake. Everyone would like that and I would make it myself. I was nineteen at the time and working at the city's new public housing community.

Thanks to our family friend Sam Gaylord, Steubenville received the government funding to build duplexes and fourplexes at the top of a hill near the local college. Sam had a real desire to help the disadvantaged and he was the only reason that I had a summer job. I don't think he knew how limited my skills were. He didn't ask if I could type and I didn't volunteer that information. I was, however, a good speller and could memorize a few lines and use the hunt and peck method.

Because of Sam my job was never in danger and in my third summer I was sent out into the neighborhood to inspect the apartments to verify that they were being well cared for. This was even crazier than having to pretend I could type. I didn't have to do much at home besides dry the dishes and make my bed.

As it turned out I loved my job and I got to know the people who were living at the projects. Before that I didn't know any black people other than the waiter at the Country Club and the woman who helped at my parents' parties and my classmate who was the only black student in our whole entire school.

In the summer of 1960 there was tension at the project, just as in other parts of the country. Someone came up with the idea of a party for everyone, including the staff, in the playground that adjoined the office. That would be a chance for the black and the white families to get better acquainted.

The day of the party I got busy making my dessert. My mother wasn't often a baker of cakes and she was out anyway so I found a recipe somewhere and got as far as producing a bowl full of very soupy chocolate. I didn't know where I had gone wrong but when my mother came home we decided I should go to Krogers and buy a cake.

I was excited to go to the party and I could hear the music even before I got out of the car. A band of black musicians was rockin' and rollin' and everyone was dancing – the little kids too – and there was food on a long table that had room for my chocolate cake.

I looked around and saw that there was only one white family there and a few of the workers from the all white office staff. Because of my "inspections", I knew most everyone there and so I stayed for a few hours on that hot summer evening and I laughed and danced and played with the little kids. I hoped that change was in the air and that a new generation would somehow fix everything. It didn't happen in the project, but even so, the party that night stayed with me forever.

Jazz Station Pumpkin Cheesecake

I always wanted to work in a restaurant and, when I was 52 years old, I applied for a job at a little café in Eugene. It was open for breakfast, lunch and dinner and also provided some very nice catering in the community. The job involved everything from cooking to doing dishes to waiting on customers and it came with the usual low wage and no benefits other than that I loved it. Some of my friends thought I had finally lost my mind but I met some wonderful people there, the most memorable being Ed Little Crow, a Native American who was one of the few Lakota speaking members of that community. Ed came in almost every day for breakfast and stayed a while. I really wanted to know more about him and, when we weren't busy, I would sit with him. He told me about his life and his family and his aunt who refused the government offer to buy her piece of land in the Black Hills. He said he went to Portland every month to speak Lakota with one of the elders there and that he spoke to groups sometimes.

I had the idea that he would be a great speaker at Bucky's Kiwanis and Bucky agreed. When the time came Ed and I showed up at the meeting. And when everyone rose to say the Pledge of Allegiance and sing America the Beautiful, Ed remained seated. He was introduced and began by referring to America as Your United States of America and I didn't even want to look around. Ed continued with stories of his aunt and the burial grounds that had been desecrated and about the agents coming to take him to jail because he hadn't registered for the draft. He talked about the Lakota and land that had been taken away and how he felt about this country that he felt no loyalty to.

I wasn't sure what the people in that room were thinking but there had to be all kinds of reactions. When Ed finished, they stood and applauded and several came up to tell me they weren't happy when Ed didn't honor the flag and the pledge but now they understood why. And they said thank you.

This is a recipe from The Jazz Station that won an award for Best Dessert at a Chef's Night Out in Eugene.

You Will Need:

For the Crust:

⅓ cup brown sugar

1 cup flour

½ cup finely chopped walnuts

½ cup melted butter

For the Filling:

24 ounces cream cheese (softened)

1¼ cups sugar

4 large eggs

1½ teaspoons vanilla

1¼ cups pumpkin puree (canned is fine)

1 teaspoon ground cloves

For the Topping:

2 cups sour cream

½ cup sugar

½ teaspoon vanilla

1 teaspoon cinnamon

1 teaspoon allspice

½ teaspoon ginger

½ teaspoon cardamom

3 tablespoons brandy

Note:

This will seem easier if you do some of it ahead of time. Combine the spices in a small jar as far ahead as you like. Also, combine the dry ingredients for the crust ahead of time and add the butter when you are ready to assemble the cheesecake.

Again, when you are making something that requires a spice or herb that you don't ordinarily use, buy a small amount at the bulk food section of the grocery store. It is extraordinarily inexpensive to do this in comparison to buying the already packaged variety and I also believe that the herbs are fresher. Also, if you don't have use for a large bottle of brandy, you can buy a tiny bottle (airline size) of it at the liquor store. It will be sufficient for making this cheesecake twice.

To make the crust, mix together brown sugar, flour, walnuts and melted butter. Press this mixture on the bottom and partway up the sides of a 9" springform pan. Bake until slightly set, about 10 minutes at 350.

For the filling, in the large bowl of your mixer, beat cream cheese, sugar, eggs and vanilla until the mixture is very smooth.

In a separate bowl, whisk pumpkin puree, cloves, nutmeg, allspice, ginger, cardamom, cinnamon and brandy. Add this to the creamed mixture and beat just until well blended.

Pour into baked crust and smooth top. Bake at 350 degrees for 50 to 60 minutes until edges are slightly browned.

Remove cheesecake from the oven and top with the mixture of sour cream, sugar and vanilla. Bake again for 10 minutes.

Cool at room temperature, then refrigerate in the pan for several hours or overnight. I place a large plate over top to be sure nothing touches the topping.

Plain Ol' Cheesecake

Note:

This cake freezes well. I freeze it in the springform pan, covered but with the plastic not touching the cake itself. Then, as soon as the cake is hardened, I remove it from the pan and wrap it in plastic wrap and then in foil. The topping will not be disturbed by the wrapping. When ready to use it, unwrap it while it is still hard to keep the topping smooth.

I usually prepare my graham cracker crumbs in the food processor. Or, if you don't have one, put the graham crackers in a tightly closed plastic zip bag and run a rolling pin over them until they are crumbs. I keep 2 or 3 containers of crumbs on hand measured out in 2 cup amounts.

Occasionally you may have the topping split a little as it cools. A quick fix for that is some strategically placed berries. This cake is always a hit no matter what.

This is a basic cheesecake with a subtle taste—a little almond, a little lemon. It was requested often when I did catering events.

You Will Need:

2 cups graham cracker crumbs

½ cup melted butter

2 pounds cream cheese, softened

1 cup sugar

1 teaspoon vanilla

½ teaspoon almond extract

2 large eggs

2 cups sour cream (light sour cream works)

½ cup sugar

½ teaspoon almond extract

Juice of half a lemon

For the Crust: Combine melted butter with graham cracker crumbs and press on bottom and a little up the sides of a lightly greased 9" or 10" springform pan. Crust does not have to be baked before filling.

For the Filling: In large bowl of mixer, beat cream cheese until smooth and add sugar, vanilla, and almond extract. Beat until well combined. Add eggs and continue beating, just enough to thoroughly combine, being careful that the mixture does not get runny.

Pour into crust, smooth out and bake in top half of the oven at 350 for 30 minutes until lightly brown. While it is baking, mix together the sour cream, sugar, almond extract and lemon juice.

Remove the cheesecake from the oven and top it with the sour cream mixture. Spread the topping to the edge. Bake 10 minutes more.

To serve, cut the cheesecake into 16 wedges – a little goes a long way. It is nice with a thick berry syrup or sliced berries for the topping.

Frozen Chocolate Cheesecake

You Will Need:

2 cups chocolate cookie crumbs

½ cup melted butter

8 ounces softened cream cheese

½ cup sugar

1 teaspoon vanilla

2 egg yolks

8 ounces semisweet chocolate, melted

2 egg whites

⅓ cup sugar

1 cup heavy cream

Mix the cookie crumbs with the butter and press into the bottom and a bit up the sides of a 9-10" springform pan. Bake in a 350 degree oven for 10 minutes, watching carefully.

For the filling: In large mixing bowl combine cream cheese, ½ cup sugar and vanilla. Blend in egg yolks. Add melted semisweet chocolate to mixture and continue blending until well combined.

In another bowl, beat egg whites until stiff, gradually adding ⅓ cup sugar. Fold into chocolate batter. Beat heavy whipping cream until soft peaks form and fold this into batter also. Folding it completely and gently is very important so you must be patient with it. A large rubber spatula works well.

Pour mixture into the baked crust and freeze covered overnight or for several days. Be sure that the plastic wrap doesn't disturb the top of the cheesecake.

To serve, remove from freezer about thirty minutes before you need it. Run a knife around the edge and remove sides of pan.

Note:

This is a version of cheesecake that has a milder chocolate flavor. Our girls like it but it comes with a warning. It calls for uncooked eggs so if you are not sure of your egg source the other chocolate cheesecake in this book would be your best bet.

You may want to whip up some more heavy cream and sweeten it with a few tablespoons of sugar. After removing from freezer, top cake with the whipped cream. It looks especially nice if you force it through a decorating tube around the edge. Add a sprinkling of sliced almonds or chopped walnuts or even some leftover crumbs that you didn't need for the crust.

Creamy Coconut Cheesecake

This is a recently discovered recipe that I changed to use a bit less coconut. The chocolate topping is optional. It is very good either way.

You Will Need:

For the Crust:

¾ cup flour

1 tablespoon sugar

6 tablespoons cold butter, cut in small pieces

For the Filling:

24 ounces cream cheese, softened

1½ cups sugar

4 large eggs

1½ cups flaked coconut

1 cup whipping cream

1 teaspoon fresh lemon juice

½ teaspoon vanilla

½ teaspoon almond extract

For the crust, combine flour and sugar and cut in butter with a food processor or pastry blender. Process until the mixture can be formed into a ball. Refrigerate about 30 minutes.

Press crust mixture into bottom and a bit up the sides of a 10" springform pan. Bake at 325 for 15-20 minutes, checking occasionally until it is golden, not brown.

For the filling, beat the cream cheese and sugar until smooth. Add in the eggs, one at a time, and beat until well combined. Beat in coconut, making sure there are no clumps, then the whipping cream, lemon juice and the extracts.

Bake for about an hour. The cake will be lightly golden and a bit jiggly when you take it out of the oven.

Let it cool completely, then refrigerate. If you freeze it for later use, let it harden in the pan and then wrap it in plastic wrap and foil.

To serve, you can top it with toasted coconut or a chocolate glaze. The one in this book with the Glazed Chocolate Cake is very good and easy.

Note:

Coconut is another item I buy in the bulk food section of the market. The packaged product contains more than I use and is also more expensive and may dry out in storage.

TWO ANGELS AND A CAKE

Have you ever baked an Angel Food Cake? The first time I had this experience was when I was spending the night at my Godparents' house. I was eight years old and, since their three sons were grown and gone from the house, they had more time to spend with me. All of the kids I knew had godparents

but I felt like the luckiest of all. Comare (Italian for godmother) Mary and Giustine were wonderful and on occasion I was able to spend the night at their house.

On one stayover, Comare Mary decided that she and I would make an Angel Food Cake and since I had never made any kind of cake, my part was just whipping the egg whites and sugar and licking the beaters afterwards. That was about it. I liked watching her and listening to her talk because she was funny but then when she put the cake in the oven I went out to the back porch to sit with Giustine.

He was a sweet, sweet man who just happened to be "stone deaf" as the grownups said. We sat and he smiled a lot and I smiled back and he sometimes patted my head and asked if I wanted to pick some of his Concord grapes. We did that together and we sat some more and ate the grapes that are my favorites to this day. I couldn't really say anything to him but I didn't talk much anyway. I was comfortable just being with him.

Giustine and I had a few adventures on my visits there. He had a big bowl of pennies and he told me to put both of my hands in the bowl and take as many as I could hold. I stuffed them in my pockets and we went for a walk. He held my hand as we travelled several blocks to Losey's Bar, a nice little neighborhood establishment, and he took me around to the side door. And there it was, a beautiful gumball machine that, besides gum, also held little silver charms. Giustine stood there and waited until I put every single penny in that machine. My pockets were really full and so was my mouth and we walked home, both of us happy as can be.

Giustine was retired but he did some clean up work at the bar that his son Porky managed. One day he and I went downtown in his car and we parked in front of the bar. We went in the back door to see Porky and entered a room that was full of tables and chairs and there were men erasing numbers and writing in new ones on a big blackboard. Phones were ringing and being answered quickly. Porky whisked us out of there and, at the time, I didn't know why. Except for the phones the place didn't look much different than a classroom at school with the chalk board and all. I liked it but I guess Porky wasn't expecting both of us.

Back to the cake. I remember that it almost melted in my mouth like nothing I had ever had. So on one of my days of reminiscing about these two fine people, I decided to make a real Angel Food Cake. It was just OK, not great. Turns out, I needed my Comare by my side.

Gingerbread

This is an old fashioned recipe and one that has a nice texture and very good flavor. It is very fast and simple to make and is a nice warm treat on a cold fall day.

You Will Need:

2½ cups flour

½ teaspoon salt

2 teaspoons baking soda

½ teaspoon ground cloves

¼ teaspoon cinnamon

1 teaspoon ginger

1 cup boiling water

1 cup molasses (I like light but dark has a more intense flavor)

1 scant cup vegetables or canola oil

2 large eggs beaten

1 cup sugar

In a medium bowl, mix together the flour, salt baking soda and spices. Set aside.

In large mixer bowl, pour boiling water over molasses and stir until combined. Add oil and eggs and sugar and mix well. Add dry ingredients and mix until all is combined. Do not go past medium speed if you are using a mixer so that the batter will have more of a hand stirred consistency.

Pour into a greased and floured 9x13" pan and bake at 350 degrees for about 35 minutes. Do not over bake but be sure the tester comes out clean. Remove from oven and cool until just warm. I do not turn this cake out of the pan because I cut it in squares for serving.

Note:

Because I can't seem to decide if I like this made with light or dark molasses I use half of each, saving my decision making for more crucial things.

When you think the cake is done, test it with a long wooden skewer that enables you to reach the cake without pulling the rack out into the cooler air. The skewers that come packaged for kabobs are perfect for this. You can wipe them off and use them several times.

I like to serve this warm but it's still good when it has cooled off. You may want to top each serving with a spoonful of lemon curd, applesauce or whipped cream.

Pineapple Upside Down Cake

Baking this cake in a springform pan makes it a whole lot easier to turn onto a platter without disturbing the topping. It is a very pretty cake and also wonderfully moist and delicious.

You Will Need:

For the Topping:

6 tablespoons unsalted butter, melted

1 tablespoon rum, dark or light

½ cup packed brown sugar

7 slices canned pineapple, juice drained and set aside

12-14 walnut halves

Dried cranberries or cherries to fill in pineapple centers

For Batter:

3 slices canned pineapple

1 tablespoon rum

½ cup margarine, softened

¾ cup sugar

2 large eggs

1 teaspoon vanilla

2 cups flour

½ teaspoon ground ginger

1½ teaspoons baking soda

½ teaspoon salt

½ cup reserved pineapple juice

Heavy cream, whipped and sweetened

Mix together the melted butter and 1 tablespoon rum and pour into a 9 inch springform pan. Distribute the brown sugar evenly over the butter and press in. Arrange the 7 pineapple slices over the brown sugar and fill in the holes with dried cranberries or cherries and the other spaces with walnut halves. Set aside.

Puree the 3 remaining pineapple slices with 1 tablespoon rum and set aside.

In a large mixer bowl cream the margarine and sugar until well combined and then beat in the eggs one at a time. Beat in the vanilla and the pureed pineapple slices.

In a smaller bowl, stir together flour, ginger, baking soda and salt. Beat this into the batter mixture alternately with the ½ cup of reserved pineapple juice. Carefully pour the batter over the pineapple slices in the springform pan.

Bake for 35 minutes in a 350 oven or until the top of the cake springs back when gently touched. After a few minutes, remove the sides of the pan and invert the cake onto a serving plate.

Note:

Room temperature is fine but this cake is especially good when served while warm with a big spoonful of sweetened whipped cream over top.

Carrot Cake

One difference in this recipe from others I have tried is that the carrots are first cooked and mashed. I use a potato masher so that there are still little pieces of carrot in the cake. It is a very rich dessert, especially with the cream cheese frosting, and it is the best carrot cake I have tasted.

You Will Need:

2 cups flour

2 cups sugar

2 teaspoon cinnamon

2 teaspoons baking soda

1 cup corn or canola oil

3 large eggs

2 teaspoons vanilla

1⅓ cups mashed cooked carrots

1 cup chopped walnuts

1 cup shredded sweetened coconut

¾ cup canned crushed pineapple, drained

In large mixer bowl, combine flour, sugar, baking soda and cinnamon. In another bowl, mix together oil, eggs and vanilla and pour this into dry ingredients. Beat on medium speed until well combined. Add remaining ingredients and mix on low speed.

Pour batter into two 8" round cake pans that have been greased and lined with waxed paper or parchment. Bake at 350 for 45-50 minutes, until a tester comes out clean.

Cool cakes on racks for fifteen minutes. Remove from pans and continue to cool.

At this point you can frost them with cream cheese frosting. You will find a recipe for the frosting following the Banana Cake recipe.

Note:

This can be stacked as a two layer cake but if I am serving several desserts I usually freeze one layer for later use. Swirl the frosting on the top of a single layer and sprinkle it with coconut-toasted or not— or slivered almonds.

Jane's Husband Ken's Aunt's Banana Cake

My friend Jane gave me this recipe when our children were small and a few years ago I told her that I have probably used it hundreds of times. She said it wasn't hers but her aunt's so, at that time, I changed the title from Jane's Banana Cake to Jane's Aunt's Banana Cake. Then recently I laughed about changing it and she said "No, it was Ken's aunt not mine." So, in the interest of accurate historical reporting, I changed it to its present title and, until I hear otherwise from the Knowlton family, it will remain that way.

I met Jane and Nancy at the pre-school that Cristianne attended when she was three and four years old. Nancy wasn't an only child but her three brothers were almost fully-grown when she was born. The pre-school was a co-op and parents were required to help out there on a rotating basis. Nancy was the sweetest child I ever met, a little shy, and we were all drawn to her. She became like another daughter to us. Jane and her family included Cristianne in their trips so that Nancy would have a playmate. She became the only one in our family who knew what camping was!

You Will Need:

⅔ cup shortening (I use butter flavor Crisco)

1½ cups sugar

2 large eggs

2 cups flour

¾ teaspoon baking powder

½ teaspoon salt

¾ teaspoon baking soda

1 cup ripe banana (very well mashed)

¼ cup buttermilk

1 teaspoon vanilla

In a large mixer bowl, cream together the shortening and sugar. Add eggs and beat well until fluffy.

You can also make cupcakes but you will have to shorten the baking time.

If you don't have buttermilk you can use sour milk. Just add a small bit of lemon juice or vinegar to whole milk or 2% and let it sit a few minutes until it curdles.

In a separate bowl, mix together flour, baking powder, salt, baking soda. In another bowl combine mashed banana, buttermilk and vanilla.

Add these two mixtures gradually and alternately to creamed mixture. Divide between two greased 8" or 9" round pans lined with parchment or waxed paper. Smooth tops and bake at 350 for about 30 minutes. For most cakes I find that the lower middle rack works best.

Check with a cake tester and remove from oven when tester comes out clean. Cool on rack for ten minutes, loosen around the edge of pan and turn out on racks.

When cool, frost with cream cheese frosting.

Cream Cheese Frosting

You Will Need:

1 8-ounce package cream cheese, softened

½ stick softened butter

3 cups powdered sugar

1 teaspoon vanilla

Half and half, enough to achieve spreading consistency

Beat the cream cheese and butter until they are well combined and then gradually add powdered sugar and vanilla. Beat well while adding half and half, a little at a time until it is of spreading consistency. I like to whip it on high speed for a minute to lighten it up. Be careful not to add too much liquid but, if you do, just add a bit more powdered sugar to tighten it up.

If you are using some of the frosting to force through a decorating tube save about ¾ cup of it out. Add some powdered sugar to firm it up some. If you have extra frosting, it will keep well in the refrigerator for several weeks.

Buttermilk Cake

Notes:

This cake is very tender so, if you are making a layer cake, handle the layers gently when stacking. Chocolate frosting or a fluffy vanilla frosting or even 7-Minute frosting all work well.

Cake flour has a finer texture than all purpose flour and adds to the tenderness of the cake. I buy it in the bulk food section of the market because I don't use it often and this allows me to buy the amount I need at a significantly lower price without sacrificing quality. If you are using all-purpose flour use ¼ cup less as it is a heavier product.

This is a recipe that I have had since I was first married. A friend of our family gave it to me and, since I was still at the "new bride" cooking stage, the ease of preparation matched my level of expertise. I actually changed the proportions a bit after I gained enough confidence to do that. It retained its tenderness but gained a little more firmness.

I made this cake for my daughter's wedding. I have cake pans of all sizes so the batter worked well for the three tiers. There are charts that can help you to choose the right pans. "The Food Lover's Companion" is the best one I have found.

You Will Need:

½ cup butter

¼ cup shortening

1½ cups sugar

3 large eggs

3 cups cake flour, sifted

1 teaspoon baking soda

1½ teaspoon baking powder

½ teaspoon salt

1¼ cups buttermilk

2 teaspoons vanilla

In a large mixing bowl, cream butter and shortening with sugar. Add eggs and beat until fluffy.

In a separate bowl, combine sifted cake flour, baking soda and baking powder. Add this to the creamed mixture alternately with buttermilk. When the mixture is light and smooth, beat in vanilla.

Pour batter into parchment or waxed paper lined baking pans. You can use a 9x13" pan or two 8"or 9" pans or cupcake tins.

Bake at 350 for about 30 minutes. 20-25 minutes if making cupcakes.

Poppy Seed Torte

I really like this cake—it is very light, similar to a sponge cake. You will end up with four thin layers. I have three different fillings in this book and all will work well for this, although the strawberry one may have to be thinned a little. If you are using the custard between the layers, you may want to spread a thin layer of raspberry jam, for flavor, on the layers first.

You Will Need:

¼ cup poppy seeds

¾ cup milk

¾ cup butter, softened

1½ cups sugar

2 teaspoons vanilla

2 cups cake flour, sifted

2½ teaspoons baking powder

¼ teaspoon salt

4 egg whites, at room temperature

In a small bowl, soak poppy seeds in milk for one hour.

In large mixer bowl, cream butter and slowly add sugar. Continue beating until fluffy. Blend poppy seed mixture into batter.

Combine cake flour, baking powder and salt. Add this to the creamed mixture, mixing until blended. Beat egg whites until stiff and gently fold these into the batter, ½ at a time.

Line two 8" round pans with parchment or waxed paper and lightly grease. Divide batter evenly between the pans and smooth tops. Bake at 375 for 20-25 minutes. Remove from oven when cake tester comes out clean. After 10 minutes, turn cakes out onto racks and peel off paper.

Cool completely then cut each layer in half horizontally. If you are worried about getting an even cut, push 6 toothpicks at intervals a little way into the sides of the cake and halfway up each layer. Slice with a sharp serrated knife.

Poppy seeds can get old so throw out the ones that have been hanging around in your cupboard for years and buy the amount you need in the bulk section of your grocery store. Okay, I won't repeat my speech about buying in bulk for freshness and economy.

If you are using the lemon curd filling, you can use two of the egg yolks that you have separated out from this recipe for the preparation of the curd.

Stack layers with filling of your choice in between layers. Cover with plastic wrap and refrigerate. This will allow the cake to firm up with the filling. You can leave it overnight if you would like.

Before it is served, the cake can be frosted in several ways. It is very good with the cream cheese frosting that is in this book. A lighter frosting would be about 2 cups of heavy cream flavored with vanilla and sweetened with 3-4 tablespoons of sugar. Beat this at high speed until stiff peaks form, being careful that you don't whip it into butter. A third and very simple topping is to use a generous sprinkling (through a sieve) of powdered sugar.

Glazed Chocolate Cake

This is a beautiful and very delicious cake. I hope you will try it.

You Will Need:

3 ounces unsweetened chocolate, chopped

1 cup boiling water

1 stick butter, cut in pieces

1½ teaspoons vanilla

2 cups sugar

2 large egg yolks, slightly beaten

2 cups minus 2 tablespoons flour

1 teaspoon baking powder

2 large egg whites

In a large bowl, pour boiling water over chopped unsweetened chocolate and butter. Stir and let stand until melted. Then stir in vanilla and sugar. Whisk in egg yolks, blending until all ingredients are well incorporated.

In a smaller bowl, mix together flour and baking powder. Add this to the chocolate mixture and mix thoroughly. Beat egg whites until stiff and then gently but thoroughly fold them into the batter, half at a time.

Grease and flour an angel food cake pan, pour the batter in and level it.

Bake at 350 degrees for 40-50 minutes on a lower middle rack until a cake tester comes out clean.

Cool for 15-20 minutes, run a knife around the edge and around the center to loosen it and turn out the cake onto a rack. Cool completely before frosting. To keep overnight, cover well with plastic wrap.

When the cake is cool, frost with the following recipe.

Chocolate Frosting

You Will Need:

2 tablespoons butter

¾ cup semisweet chocolate chips

6 tablespoons heavy cream

1 teaspoon vanilla

1¼ cups sifted powdered sugar

In a saucepan over low heat, whisk together butter, chocolate chips, heavy cream, vanilla and powdered sugar.

Place the cake on a rack with waxed paper underneath. Working quickly pour warm frosting over top of cake and, using an offset spatula, spread it gently to cover top and sides of cake. You can slide it towards the edges and then smooth it onto sides and also let some run into the center opening.

To serve, transfer to a cake plate. To do this slide a large thin metal spatula under the cake and then pull it onto the plate.

Scrape the frosting from the waxed paper into a bowl and add enough powdered sugar to make it firm enough to hold up in a decorating bag. If you have any small cracks in the frosting after transferring the cake to the serving plate, you can cover them with some swirls or dots using the frosting in the pastry bag. Make a little bouquet of flowers, a bit taller than the cake, wrap it in a wet paper towel and then wrap foil around this. Put the bouquet in center hole of cake and scatter some fresh flowers around bottom edge of cake.

Totally Beautiful & Delicious Rum Cake

This is actually a very light dessert. It is comprised of a sponge cake that is flavored after baking with a bit of rum (your choice of how much) and topped with whipped cream and fresh berries. You could make it without the rum if you are serving children.

You Will Need:

6 large eggs

1¾ cups sugar

½ cup water

2 teaspoons vanilla

2 cups cake flour

2 teaspoons baking powder

½ teaspoon salt

Rum dark or light

For Pastry Cream you can use the recipe for Custard filling in this book.

For Topping:

2 cups heavy whipping cream

¼ cup sugar

2 teaspoons vanilla

Fresh strawberries or raspberries or others of your choosing

Line a greased 12x18" baking pan with greased waxed paper or parchment.

In large mixer bowl beat 6 eggs until light and lemon colored. Gradually add the 1¾ cups sugar, beating until thick. Beat in ½ cup water and the vanilla. In a small bowl mix together the cake flour, baking powder and salt. Fold this into the egg mixture very gently and when it is nicely combined spread it evenly in baking pan. This is where an offset spatula comes in handy.

You can simplify this in a major way if you prepare the pastry cream one evening and the next day make the cake. When the cake cools assemble it with the cream and refrigerate again. The day of serving all you will have to do is whip the cream and decorate the cake. Easy.

Bake at 350 for 12-15 minutes, just until golden and a bit springy to the touch. Remove from oven and cool for 2 minutes. Loosen cake around edges if necessary and turn it out onto a smooth towel on which you have sifted flour. When cake is cooled slice it in half once crosswise and once lengthwise so that you have four pieces that are 6x9".

To assemble the cake, place one layer on your serving plate and brush the top of it with rum and then spread some of the pastry cream on that. Arrange thinly sliced strawberries or raspberries on top and continue with the other layers. The top layer will not have any of the cream on it. At this point you can tightly cover the cake and leave it overnight in the refrigerator.

To serve, cover it with a generous layer of whipped cream and then use a pastry bag to pipe on a decorative border. Arrange berries on top as you desire and scatter some around the base.

Lemon Filling

This lemon curd is quite tart. It makes enough to spread between the layers of a four layer cake.

You Will Need:

¾ cup sugar

3½ tablespoons cornstarch

¼ teaspoon salt

¾ cup water

2 large egg yolks, beaten

1 tablespoon butter

⅓ cup fresh lemon juice

1 tablespoon lemon zest, finely grated

In a small saucepan, mix together sugar, cornstarch and salt. Stir in water. Cook and stir over medium heat until thick and bubbly. Stir some of mixture into egg yolks and then return this mixture to saucepan. Heat to boiling and then boil and stir for about 5 minutes. Remove from heat and stir in butter, lemon juice and lemon zest. Cool completely before using. If refrigerating, place waxed paper directly on surface of pudding to keep a skin from forming.

Custard Filling

You Will Need:

½ cup sugar

1½ tablespoon cornstarch

4 egg yolks

1½ cups whole milk

1½ teaspoons vanilla

Lemon zest optional

In small saucepan, mix together sugar and cornstarch. In a bowl, beat together egg yolks with milk and gradually stir this into sugar mixture. Cook over medium heat until mixture thickens and boil for 1 minute. Remove from heat and stir in vanilla. Let cool and refrigerate before using. Place waxed paper directly on top of custard so that a skin doesn't form on top. Stir in a teaspoon or two of lemon zest at this time if desired.

Strawberry Cream Filling

You Will Need:

16 ounces cream cheese, softened

1¼ cups sugar

½ cup butter

1 tablespoon corn syrup

2 teaspoons vanilla

1 cup fresh strawberries, chopped

Using a mixer, beat together cream cheese with sugar and butter. After these are well combined, beat in corn syrup and vanilla and then beat in chopped strawberries.

Note:

This filling freezes well so I'd recommend making lots of it during strawberry season. A big spoonful is delicious on top of a slice of pound cake. It works well as a filling for a jelly roll cake or between the layers of the Buttermilk or Rum Cake.

Plum Tart

I like the rustic look of this. If you are not confident of your ability to make a fluted pie crust, this is an easy substitute.

You Will Need:

1 cup flour

3 tablespoons sugar

¼ teaspoons salt

½ cup cold unsalted butter

2 large egg yolks

7-8 plums, each cut into 8 wedges

4 tablespoons sugar, evenly divided

¼ teaspoon cinnamon

1 egg white, beaten with a little water

For the Crust: Combine flour, sugar and salt. Cut in ½ cup cold butter. If you are using salted butter, just use a pinch of salt. Add egg yolks and work them in until mixture holds together. Do not work it too much as that is what makes your pie dough tough. Form into a disk and refrigerate at least 30 minutes.

For the Filling: line a baking sheet with buttered foil. Place plums on the pan and sprinkle with 2 tablespoons sugar. Bake at 400 for about 20 minutes. Cool slightly.

Roll dough to a 12" round and transfer it to a large baking sheet. Leaving about a 3" margin overlap the plum slices, forming a 9" circle and working towards the center of the dough. Mix 2 tablespoons sugar with cinnamon and sprinkle over plums. Fold edges of pastry over plum filling. The dough will only partially cover the plums and will form a ragged crust. Brush the crust with the beaten egg white.

Bake until golden in a 400 oven—25 minutes or so.

Remove from oven and leave on baking sheet to cool awhile. While still slightly warm, transfer to a serving plate.

Note:

Freestone plums, such as Italian prune plums, are easiest to use because the pit is easily removed and they can be cut in even slices for a very nice effect. You can also use fresh peaches which would not need to be prebaked.

Banana Cream Pie

You are going to love this pie. It is smooth and delicious and very banana-y.

For me, it always brings to mind the times, many years ago, when my girls were very young and we would shop for school clothes at the old Bon Marche in downtown Eugene. At the time it was the only store with a children's department other than Penney's and Sears and, even though it was a department store, it had a small town feel to it. I would take the girls, one at a time, to choose a few outfits for school and we always had the same sweet woman to help us. It was special for them but probably more so for me.

The Bon had a small restaurant in the basement where we could go for lunch or a treat. I don't recall the menu so much but I do remember that they had the best banana cream pie in the world. I wasn't so forward then and didn't ask for the recipe, assuming it wasn't possible to get it. And when the Bon moved to a newly opened shopping center and went a little upscale, the café was no more.

A few years passed and there, in the Register Guard, was a recipe for banana cream pie that seemed like it might just be pretty good. I couldn't wait to try it and one taste convinced me that it was the one from the old Bon. Who knows? I will pass it along as though it were.

You will need a baked pie crust, so just use one that works for you or the one in this book with the Apple Pie recipe (for one crust, I cut it down to 1½ cups flour). I prefer the pastry type crust but you can also use a crumb crust, chocolate or graham cracker one.

You Will Need:

1 Baked pie crust

⅓ cup sugar

3 tablespoons cornstarch

¼ teaspoon salt

1½ cups whole milk

2 large eggs, separated

2 tablespoons unsalted butter, cut in small pieces

2 teaspoons vanilla

Note:

Egg whites reach a greater volume if you bring them down to room temperature before beating. The whipping cream, on the other hand, is just the opposite. Make sure the cream and the beaters and the bowl are all cold and you will achieve a better result. Just remember, the next step past the stiff peak stage is butter.

¼ cup sugar

2 thinly sliced bananas

1½ cups heavy cream, sweetened to taste

For the Filling: Combine in a saucepan, cornstarch and salt (just a pinch if you are using salted butter). Blend in whole milk and the 2 egg yolks, slightly beaten. Cook and stir over medium heat until thickened and bubbly. Remove from heat and stir in butter and vanilla. Cool to room temperature, placing plastic wrap or waxed paper right on top to keep a skin from forming.

Beat the 2 egg whites, adding ¼ cup sugar gradually until stiff peaks form. Fold into egg yolk mixture.

Spread a layer of this custard on the bottom of crust and then top this with thinly sliced bananas. Add another layer of cream and bananas, then a final layer of cream. Top with sweetened heavy cream, whipped enough to form stiff peaks. Make this early enough in the day so that the filling will firm up before serving.

It will keep well overnight too.

Sour Cream Lemon Pie

This recipe is much easier than the traditional Lemon Meringue Pie and I think the texture and the flavor are better too.

You can either use a standard pie shell for this or a graham cracker pie crust. Either way, the crust would be baked and cooled before assembling the pie. The recipe for pie crust in this book is excellent – cut it down to 1½ cups flour for one crust. The graham cracker crust with the cheesecake recipe is great too—just bake it for a short time to set it.

You Will Need:

1 cup sugar

¼ cup cornstarch

3 large egg yolks

1 cup milk, whole or 2%

¼ cup butter, cut in pieces

¼ cup fresh lemon juice

1 tablespoon finely grated lemon zest

1 cup sour cream

1½ cup heavy whipping cream, sweetened to taste

For the Filling: Mix sugar and cornstarch in a saucepan. Add egg yolks, milk, butter, lemon juice and lemon zest.

Cook and stir over medium heat until thick. Transfer to a bowl, then cool a bit before refrigerating. Refrigerate with waxed paper placed directly on top of lemon mixture to prevent a skin from forming. When completely cooled, fold in 1 cup sour cream until completely incorporated. Pour this into the pie shell.

Chill at least 4 hours before serving. To serve, top with whipped heavy cream. Try piping the stiffly beaten cream through a pastry bag with a decorative tip for a more special presentation.

Perfect Apple Pie

AN APPLE A DAY, ESPECIALLY FOR DESSERT

There is really some truth in that old adage about apples. The melatonin in them helps to regulate your metabolism and, though I can't say it keeps the doctor away, an apple a day certainly can't hurt. I also read that when flying from one time zone to another the beverage of choice should be apple juice. It helps to adjust your body clock.

Two weeks before my grandson Tucky's 8th birthday my daughter was visiting with the boys and I made this pie for dessert. All four of the grandkids were here and they all loved the pie but Tucky REALLY loved it. He decided he wanted that pie for his birthday instead of a cake. And he wanted me to make it. We talked and I said I thought he needed two pies for the number of kids coming so that was the plan. My daughter called a few days later and said he needed three pies and she would make one. I could hear him in the background saying Noni has to make them.

We went to Portland 2 days ahead of the birthday and I took with me three zip bags of the flour, sugar, salt mixture for the crust, three bags of the cinnamon, sugar, flour mixture for the apples, 3 sticks of butter and three small containers of the measured out shortening. I had fifteen large Granny Smith apples and three 9" Pyrex pie plates. I wanted the pies to be very fresh so two pies were finished the night before the party and the third was finished in the morning. I couldn't have done it without the little "do-ahead" packages. And, most importantly, Tucky was thrilled.

You will Need:

2½ cups flour

2 teaspoons sugar

1 teaspoon salt

1 stick unsalted butter, cut into small pieces

6 tablespoons cold shortening

5-6 tablespoons ice water

4-6 apples, depending on size

¾ cup sugar

1 teaspoon cinnamon

¼ teaspoon nutmeg (optional)

Dash of salt

2 tablespoons flour

2 tablespoons butter

2 tablespoons milk

Sugar for top crust

For the crust, combine 2½ cups flour, 2 teaspoons sugar and 1 teaspoon salt in food processor. Pulse a few times to mix it well. Add butter and cold shortening. Pulse until mixture is coarsely combined. Add ice water about ⅓ at a time until dough holds together. Do not process too much or it will be tough. Remove from bowl, form into 2 disks and wrap well in plastic wrap. Refrigerate at least 2 hours or even overnight.

Peel, core and thinly slice apples. Mix together about ¾ cup sugar, cinnamon, nutmeg, salt and the 2 tablespoons flour and toss apples with this mixture.

Roll out half the dough to fit a 9" pie plate. Heap apple slices in it and dot with bits of butter, using around 2 tablespoons total. Roll out remaining crust and place over apples. Seal top to bottom crust and cut slits in top. Brush with milk and sprinkle with sugar. Bake at 400 for about 50 minutes. If crust is browning too quickly, cover very loosely with a tent of aluminum foil.

Note:

If you are refrigerating the dough overnight you may want to let it sit out for about 30 minutes before rolling it out. It will soften some to make it easier to roll out.

I use Granny's because they are consistently firm and a bit tart. There are so many varieties now that you may like something different. I would stay away from the bags of little apples that are bargain priced. You will do a lot of peeling and cutting to get the same amount of filling as four or five large apples so it may not be a bargain after all.

For baking I set my pie on my round flat baking pan with fluted sides and a hole in the center. It will catch any overflow of juices and ensure that you won't have to do an oven cleanup.

Apple Squares

Our first house in Eugene had a big backyard with fruit trees and a walnut tree. This recipe was one that was going around and it was a good way, other than making applesauce, to use some of our boxes full of Gravenstein apples. It has an unusual twist with the cereal but I think that may help to produce a filling that holds together when cutting into bars.

You Will Need:

8-10 apples, thinly sliced

1 cup sugar

1 teaspoon cinnamon

½ teaspoon salt

1½ cups slightly crushed corn flakes

3 cups flour

1 teaspoon salt

1 cup shortening

2 large eggs, separated

whole or 2% milk

Peel, core and slice the apples and mix them with sugar, cinnamon and salt. Let this stand while you prepare the crust.

For the crust, mix flour with 1 teaspoon salt. Cut in shortening until mixture is crumbly. Add egg yolks beaten with enough milk to make ⅔ cup.

Work liquid into dough until it is holding together.

Divide dough in half and roll out one piece to fit an 11x15 pan. Scatter crushed corn flakes over crust. Add apples to cover. Roll out other half of dough. Place over apples and seal edges. Beat reserved egg whites with a teaspoon of water until frothy and brush on crust.

Bake at 375 for 30 minutes or until golden brown. While slightly warm, drizzle with icing. This would just be a mixture of powdered sugar with enough milk in it to allow it to be poured from a spoon. Cut into squares.

Note:

The texture of apples varies and for this recipe I prefer Gravensteins or any variety that breaks down well with cooking. The juice from the apples is absorbed by the corn flakes and the filling is soft.

Apple Fritters

I use apples cut into small chunks instead of the rings that most recipes call for. It makes for a better distribution of the fruit.

You Will Need:

1 cup plus 2 tablespoons flour

1 tablespoon sugar

A pinch of salt

1½ teaspoons baking powder

½ teaspoon cinnamon

¼ teaspoon nutmeg

1 large egg

⅔ cup milk

1 tablespoon melted butter

2 apples, not so tart, maybe Fuji

Canola oil for cooking

Powdered Sugar for sifting over top

In a large bowl, sift together flour, sugar, salt, baking powder, cinnamon, and nutmeg. In another bowl, mix together egg, milk and melted butter. Combine both mixtures and stir until just combined.

Pare 2 large apples and cut them into small pieces. Drop these into the batter and fold in to coat them. Heat two inches of canola oil to medium high in a deep pot.

Cook only as many as will fit into the pot without crowding. Using two tablespoons, scoop out some batter and drop it into oil. Cook until golden on one side then turn over to cook the other side.

Drain on paper towels and keep in a 200 oven as you finish the rest of the fritters.

Remove to a serving platter and sift powdered sugar on top.

Note:

Choose whichever apples you prefer – tart and firm or soft and sweet. I've done both and they are very good.

Peach Cobbler

This is another very simple recipe and could be doubled if you are serving a large crowd. It is especially easy if you use good quality frozen peaches that come in a large bag (you know, Costco size).

You Will Need:

Sliced peaches, 2 pounds frozen or equivalent in fresh

⅓ cup brown sugar

1 tablespoon fresh lemon juice

Scant teaspoon cinnamon

¾ cup flour

½ cup sugar

2 teaspoons baking powder

¼ teaspoon salt

¾ cup cream

½ stick melted butter

Mix together brown sugar, lemon juice and cinnamon. Toss this mixture with the sliced peaches and place them in a greased 9x13 pan.

Mix together flour, baking powder and salt. Stir in cream and butter. Drop spoonfuls of batter on top of peaches and spread it around to cover as much as you can.

Bake at 375 for 40-45 minutes, until top is golden and fruit is bubbling. Let sit until just warm and serve with whipped cream or ice cream.

BLACKBERRIES, TWO GOATS AND A PONY

Everywhere we lived in Oregon, we had blackberries. We didn't plant them and we tried our best to get rid of them but there they were. The first few years we were here, we considered ourselves lucky to have these juicy berries but when we had other ideas for the yard it became a battle that the blackberries were winning.

Every year they multiplied and whacking them down only seemed to help them along. What to do, what to do! We heard somewhere that goats were a natural solution to the problem. My friend Robin, who lived next door, liked the idea and she wanted to share the goat and also, she already had a pen for it. When we went to the goat farm the man there said that you need to have two because one alone would cry a lot. We brought two young adorable nubians home and they did love the berries. Although the goats were my idea, most of our other animals were adopted because I had a hard time saying no to our girls. We ended up with birds, hamsters, fish, bunnies, cats, dogs and most memorably, a pony named Pepe who wouldn't let anyone but Joan ride him because she was the lightest one around.

On one 90 degree day, while Bucky was conveniently out of town, I discovered that Pepe had knocked over part of his corral fencing and was gone. I called the Sheriff's Department and asked if anyone had found a pony. "Why yes", they said and gave me a phone number. The woman I contacted asked me to describe him, color, markings, location of markings. I wondered how many other people had called her about a lost pony. My patience was wearing thin when she asked how many legs had markings. I said, "Lady, if you want a pony, he's yours." She declined the offer.

A friend drove me to the woman's house, not quite a mile away, and Pepe and I started the long, hot march home with both of us at the end of our ropes. He would stop periodically and refuse to continue on.

I was pulling him and sweating and I thought of Bucky away and probably eating a nice lunch and I wondered how in the heck Pepe escaped from the so-called corral that he built. And how did I let Cristianne talk me into buying a pony and how old was this pony anyway and why was the guy at the Sand Dune Rides so eager to give him up and also deliver him all the way to Eugene from the Coast. As I dragged Pepe along, my conversations with him were not pleasant ones and with everything that had transpired, I became more certain that we were not meant for each other. The next day he became a charitable donation to a very happy 4-H group.

Blackberry Cobbler

Cobblers are so much easier than pies because there is just a batter that is spread over top of the berries. It is another comfort food, especially when it is still a bit warm when serving.

You Will Need:

6 cups blackberries

1 cup sugar

¼ cup flour

2 cups flour

1 cup sugar

1 tablespoon baking powder

1 teaspoon salt

1 cup whole milk

1 stick unsalted butter, melted

1 tablespoon cinnamon sugar

Mix one cup of sugar with ¼ cup flour in a large bowl. Add the blackberries and toss gently. Do this immediately before mixing your batter so that they do not give up too much juice.

For the batter, combine the flour, sugar, baking powder and salt in a large bowl. Stir to combine. Then add the milk and melted butter and beat until smooth, by hand or with a mixer.

Pour the berries into a 15" oval baking dish (or a 13x9" rectangular) . Drop spoonfuls of batter on top and spread around to cover the berries. Sprinkle top with cinnamon sugar.

Bake the cobbler in a 350 oven for about an hour or until the crust is golden and the berries are bubbling. Let this cool for about ½ hour and serve it just warm. You can also serve at room temperature so that the juices are not runny.

Easy & Delicious Blueberry Tart

If you are timid about making pie crust, I promise you this one is no-fail. If you are having last minute company you can easily put this together, especially if you keep a supply of blueberries in your freezer. The crust is not the roll out type. You just empty it into the pan and push it gently to the edges. It is very flaky and just sweet enough.

You Will Need:

1 cup flour

Pinch of salt

2 tablespoons sugar

½ cup butter

1 tablespoon white vinegar

2 tablespoons flour

⅔ cup sugar

¼ teaspoon cinnamon

4-5 cups blueberries

For the Crust: Mix together flour, salt and sugar. Cut in butter as for any pie crust. Sprinkle with vinegar and work dough until it comes together. Press into bottom and up the sides of a 9" tart pan with a removable bottom.

For the Filling: Mix together 2 tablespoons flour, ⅔ cup sugar and ¼ teaspoon cinnamon. Toss this well with 4 cups fresh or frozen blueberries and pour this mixture into the crust. Place pan on a baking sheet to catch any juice that might overflow and bake on the lowest rack of a 400 degree oven for about 50 minutes. The crust should be golden brown. Remove from oven and sprinkle with a few uncooked blueberries, if desired.

Serve slightly warm with freshly whipped heavy cream or ice cream.

Note:

The tart can be made with a variety of fruits. I made a delicious one using a combination of different pears from Joan and Pat's family's backyard. I used ⅓ cup of white sugar and 3 tablespoons of brown sugar and sprinkled 3 tablespoons of dried cranberries in for color. If the cranberries are quite dry, soak them in ¼ cup of apple juice for about an hour before using. Drain before adding. I have used peaches and blackberries and combos of fruit I had on hand. I honestly think you can't go wrong.

Strawberry Tarts

This recipe will make six 5" tarts. You will need the tart pans with removable bottoms. If you do not have them, you could make a single crust pie using the recipe. I would recommend using the whole pie crust recipe that is with the apple pie recipe in this book. You can refrigerate or freeze any leftover dough.

You Will Need:

Pie crust for double crust

1 quart strawberries

1 tablespoon fresh lemon juice

½ cup sugar

1 tablespoon cornstarch

8 ounces cream cheese, softened

3 tablespoons milk

1 teaspoon grated lemon zest

1 pint heavy cream for whipping, optional

2-3 tablespoons sugar

Roll out the pie crust to ⅛" thickness and fit it into a pie plate or tart pans. Bake in a 400 oven for about 8 minutes or until golden. Cool shells on wire rack. If making tarts remove them from the pans when cool.

In a saucepan crush 1 cup strawberries. Add 1 tablespoon lemon juice, sugar and cornstarch. Cook over low heat, stirring, until thickened and clear. Set aside to cool.

Mix cream cheese with 3 tablespoons milk and lemon zest until it is easy to spread. You can also force the mixture through a cake decorating bag. This will give you a very even coating of cream cheese.

Fold remaining berries into cooled berry mixture until they are all glazed. If the berries are large you may want to cut them in half. Arrange them attractively on top of the cream cheese and drizzle any remaining syrup over tops. Top each tart with whipped cream.

Lemon Ice Cream

This is a snap to make because you do not need to use an ice cream maker. It is very refreshing after a summer dinner from the grill.

You Will Need:

¼ cup fresh lemon juice

Zest of one large lemon, finely grated

1 cup sugar

1 cup whole milk

1 cup heavy cream

In a large bowl, combine the sugar, zest and lemon juice. Add milk and stir until the sugar is completely dissolved. Be very sure that there are no granules left in the mixture. In another bowl, beat the cup of cream until stiff peaks form and fold this into the sugar mixture. Pour into a 9x5x3" loaf pan lined with foil. Cover and freeze 4-5 hours or overnight. To serve, remove the whole block and slice it about ¾ inch thick or, if you prefer, using an ice cream scoop, drop it into individual dessert bowls.

This looks pretty with some raspberries scattered over top with a small flower such as a pansy or viola on the side.

Tips & Tricks

(1) Here's a pretty recent discovery. If you buy celery by the whole bunch as I do, instead of a few stalks at a time, wrap the whole thing in aluminum foil and it will stay crisp and fresh for weeks. It really works and you won't have any waste – the stalks can be used for salads or just eating, the leaves and inner stalks are perfect for soups and stews.

(2) We are fortunate to have a good market near us that has an excellent bulk food department. I buy as much as I can this way for several reasons. Most times the herbs are at least ¼ of the cost of the ones in little jars. If you rarely use a certain herb buy a small amount and freshen your supply when you need to.

(3) For years, when I would chop green or red peppers, I would halve them and pull out the seeds and break the stem off and then proceed. I saw someone do a much quicker job of it – stand the pepper up, and cut one side off and then rotate it and keep cutting the side pieces off. Voila – throw away the stem and core all in one piece.

(4) If you only use coconut for your biscotti or carrot cake or another recipe, scoop up what you actually need from the bulk bins. Buy the bulk oatmeal, nuts and dried fruit for your baking and even the sesame oil or corn meal that you use only occasionally. Everything you buy in bulk is going to be a lot less expensive than the packaged alternative and by storing it in containers that you already have on hand, it will have less of an impact on the local landfill.

(5) About ten years ago, when I was cooking for a crowd on a regular basis, I learned that you can cook bacon in the oven. Place it in a single layer on a jelly roll pan or any shallow pan with sides. You may want to line it with foil to save cleanup. Cook at 375 for about 15-20 minutes, turning the pieces once. Check occasionally – the thickness of the bacon may affect the time for baking.

(6) When you are preparing for a big holiday dinner or are just fitting some special cooking into your busy schedule, there are many things you can do in advance. Check your recipe and think for a minute about what that would be. Several days, or one day ahead you can grease and flour cake pans, combine and tightly cover dry ingredients, season and stuff a roast, prepare salad dressing, crush graham crackers for crumb crusts and the list goes on.

(7) When I was a kid, I didn't do any real cooking, just the small chores like this one. If you like fresh parsley – which is always nice as a garnish – rinse it well, shake the excess water off and pinch off the tops. Put them in a glass jar or zip bag. They will keep fresh and crisp for weeks. Tie the stems into a bundle to save for seasoning a soup or stew recipe.

(8) My kitchen is outfitted with the things I really, really use a lot. Long ago I got rid of the knives that don't hold a sharp edge, the garlic press that was just another thing to wash, the electric can opener that took up space, the extraneous pots and pans that could be used by someone else. So I am down to my tried and true equipment, some of which I am in love with—my offset small spatula that is perfect for leveling cake batter and for spreading frosting on the side of the cakes, my fine holed grater that a brilliant rasp user invented and, thanks to Cristianne, my deep, long handled, slotted scooper that is the slickest thing ever for retrieving the gnocchi or other things from boiling water and, of course, my ricer, without which there would be no gnocchi to retrieve.

(9) If you are unsure about how to store produce, you can ask the grocer or just take a look around to see how it is displayed in the store. For example, tomatoes are not in the refrigerated areas because that would stop the ripening process and the flavor would not develop. If you are buying potatoes in a five or ten pound bag, check to see that there are no signs of rot. One bad potato can infect the others. It is best to take them out of the bag and store them in a basket in a cool place, maybe your garage or basement.

10 I'm nothing if not thrifty so I encourage you to look at your second hand stores for some items. There are always very large, about 18" diameter, stainless mixing bowls to be had and they are a real help if you are making the pizza dough or cinnamon rolls or rice salad in this book. I have found beautiful high grade ceramic baking dishes and even ricers to give to friends. True, you have to look through a lot of junk to find the treasures but they are there and almost free.

11 If you stick with the essentials for the way you cook you can bypass all those little gadgets that you might use once a year. Think about what you really use. The rest may just be clutter. And, above all, take pleasure in your time in the kitchen – the tastes, the cooking smells, the feel of the ingredients and the colors of a bowl of fresh fruit or vegetables. You just can't beat it.

Index

ACKNOWLEDGMENTS

It's been a family affair, writing this book. And it has been on the back burner for many years. It came to fruition because we found Lorna Nakell and Poppy Milliken. They gave so much of their time and talents and they steered us onto the right pathways. I can't thank them enough.

Bucky (Jim) and my daughter Kathleen pulled this tech impaired person through the maze of computer land and they kept their sweet natures intact.

All of our three daughters and their husbands and our four wonderful grandkids are loving and kind and always so supportive. I do know how fortunate I am.

Many of my friends who have gathered around our dining table have been cheering me on for years. So to them I say, "I told you I was writing a cookbook!"

Recipe Notes

Recipe Notes

Made in the USA
San Bernardino, CA
22 September 2014